TREVOR DANCE has studied more than three decades and has led regular readings of Rudolf Steiner's four Mystery Dramas at Rudolf Steiner House, London, since 2010. He is a retired lecturer in adult education, where one of his finest achievements was turning GCSE students on to Shakespeare. An all-round lover of the arts, he has curated exhibitions, given talks and led study groups, and is an exhibiting printmaker and member of the Printmakers' Council. He is also the author of the monograph: *Rodolphe Bresdin: an Incorrigible Bohemian*. Trevor has a BA and MA in English Literature (from Loughborough and Lancaster universities respectively). His website is: www.trevordance.org.uk

THE MYSTERY
OF THE PORTAL

A Guide to Rudolf Steiner's first Mystery Drama

Trevor Dance

RUDOLF STEINER PRESS

Rudolf Steiner Press
Hillside House, The Square
Forest Row, East Sussex RH18 5ES

www.rudolfsteinerpress.com

Published by Rudolf Steiner Press in 2022

A catalogue record for this book is available from the British Library

ISBN 978 1 85584 597 8

Cover by Andrew Morgan Design
Typeset by Symbiosys Technologies, Visakhapatnam, India
Printed and bound by 4Edge Ltd., Essex

Contents

Acknowledgements

We all stand on the shoulders of giants. Harry Collison's, *A Commentary on Rudolf Steiner's Four Mystery Plays*, surely has to be an important source for a writer of a guide to one of these dramas, as was the wisdom of Hans Pusch, expressed in *Working Together on Rudolf Steiner's Mystery Dramas*. Eileen Hutchins's *Introduction to the Mystery Plays of Rudolf Steiner* was also helpful.

I took over the termly drama readings at Rudolf Steiner House from Philip Martyn, who worked with them for many years and knowledgeably helped many to engage with the plays. David Lowe's presentations on Goethe at Rudolf Steiner House stimulated my interest in the bard of Weimar. The Stroud Mystery Drama group's diligent work with the dramas, led by Richard Ramsbotham, has ensured the possibility of viewing them for many anthroposophists in the U.K. Those who have kept the performances being regularly staged at the Goetheanum have similarly benefitted international audiences.

My partner, Dagmar Steffelbauer, has diligently and patiently helped me in reading the drama in German/English.

My thanks to Tom Raines for the exegesis of the tale. *New View* magazine has published many fine articles on the characters, especially those of David Wood and Richard Ramsbotham, also on many related topics.

Introduction

The belief that such a guide is sorely needed has been the motivating force in the writing of this book. At the time of writing, the only sources of help available in print to anyone wishing to study the play are the brief synopses in Eileen Hutchins's, *Introduction to the Mystery Plays of Rudolf Steiner*. These are very perceptively written, but it is strange that when one studies a Shakespeare play, there is a plethora of possible aids—the study guides such as *Coles Notes*, *Methuen's Study-Aids*, *York Notes* and several other such publications; if one then wishes to further investigate, the critics themselves such as, A.C. Bradley, Northrop Frye etc. can be consulted.

The Mystery Dramas of Rudolf Steiner—plays of considerable length and complexity—seem to plead for such help to be available to those who wish to investigate their bountiful contents. *The Portal of Initiation*, is so rich in content that Steiner said:

> Everything you find in my book, *Knowledge of the Higher Worlds and its Attainment* ... combined with what was said in *Occult Science* can be found, after all, in a much more forceful, true to life, and substantial form in the Rosicrucian Mystery.[1]

Surely a guide was needed!

This book certainly is just a guide. The task of writing it was undertaken with great trepidation. Steiner was rightly scathing about commentaries on works of art:

> Abstract thoughts deaden artistic phantasy. Becoming more and more logical, one takes to writing commentaries on works of art. This is a terrible product of a materialistic age: scholars write commentaries, learned descriptions of the art of Leonardo, Raphael, Michelangelo, are coffins in which genuine artistic feeling, living art, lie buried. If one picks up a *Faust* or *Hamlet* commentary, it is like touching a corpse. Abstract thoughts have murdered the work of art.[2]

Steiner, however, loved the work of the art writer, Herman Grimm and perhaps even more pertinently assisted Harry Collison with his superb, *A Commentary on Rudolf Steiner's Four Mystery Plays*. Steiner obviously realized that such a book was needed.

The present book is designed as simply a stimulus for the reader to add to, agree or disagree with and to contradict if necessary. The way of thinking of anthroposophy, and of the drama, demands flexibility. I hope I have succeeded in being tentative enough. The guide can be read straight through or used for reference. Each section has a certain autonomy.

The understanding of Steiner's methodology as a dramatist is crucial to an appreciation and love of the plays. Why is the first scene of *The Portal of Initiation* so long? Why are many speeches so lengthy? Why are our usual expectations of a drama—that it will have us sitting on the edge of our seats anxious about the fate of the hero; it will make us laugh, or cry—why are such expectations not met?

Hopefully the exploration of these questions will facilitate a greater appreciation and enjoyment of the drama. Above all, I hope it helps readers to work with this extraordinary play. The rich mixture of Goethe's alchemical fable, 'The Green Snake and the Beautiful Lily' and the spiritual development of the individual characters ensures the uniqueness of *The Portal of Initiation*. It has an aesthetic charm, unique and resonant.

The initial chapters, prior to the investigations of the scenes and characters, set out to afford an overview of the origins of the drama and the methodology employed in its creation. 'The Birth of the Portal—A Modern Mystery Drama', sketches the origins and influences. It does not attempt to be comprehensive—one could write a whole book with such a title; however, it is helpful to see that the drama, despite its radicalism, is firmly rooted in fertile ground. 'A Portal to a Different Kind of Drama', examines Steiner's methods as a playwright. Hopefully some of the reservations the reader may have about a play which ignores so many of the normative ground rules of theatrical productions can be assuaged. Was Steiner a teacher, using the play as a teaching vehicle—a kind of visual aid? Or was he a highly competent dramatist?

There then follows a section on the scenes and a synopsis of each, focusing not simply on the plot, but also on the dramatic qualities of Steiner's work. Both are inextricably linked, and sometimes the latter is easier to misunderstand or overlook than the former.

The characters and their contributions to the drama are the next stop on our journey. They form a rich and varied gathering! The collectivity of rustics, sophisticates, hierophants and spiritual entities provide a pageant to ponder. The unity of the alchemical fable and its spiritual dimensions with the very modern characters and their faults, foibles and arid soul-centred dilemmas gives *The Portal* its flavour—a unique flavour. We are afforded the distresses and quandaries of Johannes, Maria, Capesius and Strader and transported to the other worldly realms of The Spirit of the Elements and the 'Maya Temple'.

I am very pleased to include Tom Raines's clear and perspicaciously observed essay on Goethe's tale, 'The Green Snake and the Beautiful Lily'. Although the play need not be studied with reference to Goethe's alchemical allegory, very much is gained in so doing. I have referred throughout to the 'equivalent' characters in the tale and the correspondence between the play and the tale should not present the reader with too many pitfalls.

My hope is that this guide will help to facilitate work on this wonder-filled and wonderful play and that it will be helpful to the individual reader and to study groups. The play must not be simply a part of the anthroposophical calendar. It is worthy of lifelong study; one can happily return to it year after year. The depths are never plumbed; the streams of wonder never run dry. Steiner often emphasized this need. The drama belongs to the tradition of Mystery Dramas from the ancient Mystery Centres as vehicles for advancement along the spiritual path. To cultivate a love for the drama and the alchemical fable of Goethe is to harvest a bountiful yield for soul and spirit.

A Portal to a Different Kind of Drama

'We should be aware that
this Rosicrucian Mystery contains
many of our spiritual scientific teachings
that perhaps only in future years
will be discerned.'

Rudolf Steiner[1]

Easy they are not; infinitely rewarding they are! The Mystery Dramas of Rudolf Steiner were the most radical productions ever to be staged. They remain challenging for audiences today. Dramas that can be watched an infinite number of times with no law of diminishing returns setting in; these Mystery Dramas impel us to return not only to performances, but to many a serious perusal of the text.

Our normal theatre-going habits are constantly challenged by the dramas. The expectation of a pleasing two or three hours at the theatre, followed by drinks or a pleasant meal, is out of sync with a performance lasting six or seven hours. There is little outright laughter, still less are tears brought to our eyes. We do not sit on the edge of our seats worrying what will happen next. It is probably for these reasons that Steiner was reluctantly impelled to express surprise and disappointment at the reticence of his pupils:

> In various places since the performance of the drama in Munich, I have stated the fact that many, many things of an esoteric nature would not need to be described, that lectures would be unnecessary on my part, if only everything that lies in the Rosicrucian Mystery could work directly on your souls, my dear friends, and on the souls of others too. I would have to use the enormous number of words necessary in my lectures and speak for days, for weeks, even for years, in order to describe what has been said and what could be said in the single drama.[2]

One can, perhaps, sympathize with those anthroposophical pioneers of 1910, who were being thus berated. Were they previously informed that their customary habits of theatre attendance were under attack? Whilst we might, if seeing a Shakespeare play which is unfamiliar to us, or some other production that promises complexity, engage in some research beforehand to ensure we do not 'lose the plot', we do not expect to work on the play having once seen it. This we would only do if we were studying it for an exam.

'In various places', indicates Steiner's determination to change such habits. He was clearly surprised and taken aback at the lack of endeavour after the viewing of the play. Partial success has certainly ensued. Thousands have happily imbibed the bountiful fruits of wisdom in the drama. To overcome our normal expectations of a play is, however, no easy matter. Why is the seemingly interminable first scene so full of conversation and so lacking in action? Why are the speeches often so long? Why could the play itself not be wound up in the seventh scene, allowing us time for dinner and drinks? Was Steiner a wonderful teacher who just used the play as a teaching vehicle?

The answers to these questions lie in the aims and content of the drama itself. When one thoroughly examines *The Portal of Initiation*, Steiner is revealed as a highly competent dramatist. The norms of drama are often stood on their head—always deliberately, always with clarity of purpose. The first scene needs to be of such length not simply to introduce the multiplicity of engaging characters but to convincingly induce the turmoil in the soul of Johannes which leads into the following iconic Rock Spring Scene. The play focuses on the development of the characters, particularly Johannes Thomasius and requires the extra time so to do.

The Word
The word is truly the vehicle of the Mystery Drama. The desire that our cinema-going, television-watching and theatre-attending habits have cultivated for actions rather than words, has to be put on hold. This primacy of the word, utterly necessary in a contemporary spiritual drama—is the force endowing the Mystery Drama with its unique character. The whole structure of the play is word-focused. Fairy stories, prayers, mantras, argumentative dialogues, passages of sublime lyricism are interwoven in a tapestry of poetic resonance.

The Structure of the Play

The play commences with prose. The Prelude has to be prosaic. We are in the cosy, domestic interior of Sophia's room. The children sing and the first lines,

> The light of the sun is flooding
> the realms of space;[3]

echo throughout the drama—the motif of the light works through from Johannes's darkness in the second scene to the beautiful mantras of Benedictus, the light of Devachan in scene seven and on into the Sun Temple. The dialogue of the argument between Sophia and Estella, the only character openly hostile to anthroposophy, is deliberately earthy.

From this prosaic basement we are able to move through the gears as the language becomes increasingly heightened. The first scene, although consisting of conversation is afforded the gravitas of a poetic structure. The speakers are all spiritual seekers and we witness the vision of the etheric Christ. The argument of the Prelude is mirrored in the discussion between Capesius and Strader with Maria, The Other Maria, Philia, Astrid and Luna. The Rock Spring Scene, which follows, takes us directly into the poetic realm, with its rhythmic repetitions and its language of raging dragons. We ascend into the astral realm and the fairy tale in scenes four, five and six, culminating in our further ascent into Devachan and the lyricism of the conversation of Maria and her soul forces—Philia, Astrid and Luna.

We then *have* to be brought back right down to the earth. Once again it has to be Sophia's room, references to the children and an argument with her good friend. The process repeats in the second half of the play—the mirror argument in scene eight, another Rock Spring Scene and the climax in the harmony of the Sun Temple. There is a certain necessary asymmetry within the symmetry, to avoid dullness, but the structure is finely graduated—nothing is extraneous; everything contributes.

Dialogues

The Socratic style of argumentative dialogue in the Prelude, and later in the Interlude, sets the tone for discussions which occur throughout the play. These may take the form of characters openly engaging in dialectics, as in scenes one and eight, where sceptical views are pitted against those of a spiritual scientific persuasion. The interplay of opposites is, however, varied. Sometimes differing outlooks are shown side by side, rather than through argument. The juxtaposition of the Aristotelian, Strader and the Platonist, Capesius affords an overview to the audience—neither is wholly right or wrong. A similar juxtaposition allows us to engage with the different pull of each of the adversarial powers in scenes four, ten and eleven, when Lucifer and Ahriman are on stage.

Prayers and Mantras

The language of prayer and mantra *must* resonate. Strength and gravitas are ever present in Steiner's mantras and verses. There is variety too as the singing of the children in the Prelude chimes with the simple prayer Benedictus gives Maria's child. The beautiful mantric sequence of Benedictus, followed by the Spirit Voice concluding scene three, features again in the reformulation at the end of scene seven. Steiner's suggestion that this should be studied in German is followed through in Appendix 2. The point here is that as well as affording variety and contrast in the language a deepening of the mood is delicately brought about.

Thunder and Lightning

A radical use of the word occurs in scene four, in which the prosaic, destructive outpourings of Capesius and Strader cause thunder and lightning in the astral world. This highly effective piece of drama is a vivid graphic illustration of the results of academic arrogance and its effect on the spiritual and natural world.

The Soul Forces and the Devachan Scene

The allocation of the realms of the soul, which are normally intertwined in every individual, to three separate characters on stage is far from simply being an ingenious teaching device of a didactic playwright. It certainly imprints in our souls and our memories a vivid clarification of the characteristics of the sentient soul, the mind or intellectual soul and the consciousness soul. As Steiner says:

> Separated from each other, they show themselves clearly: Philia as she places herself in the cosmos; Astrid as she relates herself

to the elements; Luna as she directs herself into free deed and self-knowledge.[4]

The speeches were received by Steiner directly from the spiritual world. The beauty of this part of the seventh scene is that of words which enchant the characters and the audience. Philia, Astrid and Luna are alive as individual characters—yes, with Maria they form an egoity—but the language is that of sisterhood. They are almost as a coven of white witches—practitioners of white magic, who will inspire Johannes, but who enchant and inspire us too.

It is as a beautiful ritual that the alchemical, caressing power of this interaction commands our attention. Maria commences in the manner of an invocation:

> You my sisters, at this hour
> be once again my helpers,
> as you have often been before
> that I may make world-ether
> resound within itself.[5]

She then explains and instructs as to how they must help Johannes. Each responds with two affirmations, 'I will … I will … ' and concludes, 'that you, beloved sister … may … '.The pattern is then repeated with Maria poetically enumerating and describing their tasks, incorporating the elemental powers of the undines, sylphs and fire beings.

The order of responses is then repeated in a charming, ritual fashion with Philia entreating, 'the spirits of the worlds', Astrid guiding, 'streams of love', and Luna beseeching, 'both strength and courage'.[6]

The entry of Johannes is needed to guide us back down from the heights of such lyricism. We might wish to stay in this sublime poetic realm, but duty must call us back towards the narrative. As already mentioned the second half of the play has a similar poetic structure—rising from the basement of the Interlude to the Sun Temple, but the seventh scene is a climax of lyrical reverie.

The Play and the Fairy Tale

The Uniqueness of the Portal

The Portal of Initiation is unique even amongst Steiner's Mystery Dramas. Steiner himself described a kind of demarcation line by saying that the first two dramas were written through him and the final two were written by him. The latter do not refer to other sources, whereas *The Portal of Initiation* strongly references Goethe's tale, and *The Soul's Probation* relates to the legend of the Knights Templar at Burg Lockenhaus. Whilst in both instances those sources are skilfully and ingeniously interwoven with the play, the latter play utilizes the legend mainly in the retrospect of scenes six to nine. The harmonizing of the tale and the development of the individual characters affords *The Portal of Initiation* its uniquely enchanting atmosphere—its alchemical genius.

Rudolf Steiner affirmed that genuine fairy tales and traditional folk stories were a source of spiritual wisdom, emanating from the time of human connectivity with higher forces (the ancient clairvoyance). The wish to feature Goethe's fairy tale on a modern stage provided the original impulse for what became *The Portal of Initiation*. The attempt to do this was unsuccessful. Modernity demanded a more 'lifelike' production with 'real' characters, and so the creative process of the metamorphosis of the tale into the drama had to be accomplished. This hard edge of contemporary life, with its doubts and hardships combining with the charm of the fairy-tale elements affords *The Portal of Initiation* its wholly individual flavour.

This imagery of charm, utterly devoid of sentimentality, allows for a heightened, elevated use of language. This again is tempered with the requirements of contemporary society. Felicia's tale in scene six is a simple story—pared down with few adjectives or descriptive phrases. It is followed by the mockery of Gairman—the Spirit of the Earth Brain brings us back to earth!

For the fairy tale to become a vehicle in itself for the wisdom and artistry of the fairy-tale teller, Frau Balde, was ingenious and appropriate. The play focuses on harsh realities of contemporary life—Estella's play, *The Uprooted* with its parallels to the drama tells of 'a man of promise' who became 'a desolate ruin of one', and ended in 'utter despair'[7]—the point where the spiritual development of Johannes begins. The fairy-tale imagery of nature spirits, supernatural landscapes and other worldly beings forms an effective dramatic counterpoint to the dryness and despair of those characters suffering the aridity of modernity.

Felix and Felicia are retained in the other dramas and are a foil for the urbane professor and doctor. The charm and wit they carry is a godsend to a dramatist. There is no room, however, for others such as The Spirit of the Elements and The Other Maria. It is *The Portal of Initiation* which Steiner styled as *The Rosicrucian Play* which has this Goethean magic (and Goethean science!).

The play interestingly contrasts with the tale. As we have seen, it is the word rather than the action which forms the pivotal force of the play. The tale focuses on action. Every sentence moves the storyline along. All is plot. As an alchemical fable it has to feature a series of symbolic actions. This too adds to the potency, the richness of meaning, of the play.

Spiritual Realism

Rudolf Steiner insisted that the characters in the drama were based on real human beings. Genuine art, according to Steiner, is the attempt to bring to a level of perfection the images that are to be found in nature and in ordinary life. The artist does not start with an idea. Didacticism in art is to be avoided—as one can gauge from Estella's remarks about 'puppet-like types indulging in symbolical events'.[8]

The need for art which is based initially upon the image allows for the spiritual forces at work within the artist to carry the work into uncharted territory. Steiner wrote as the plays themselves were being rehearsed. Such a level of spontaneity ensured a creative buzz of energy and full-hearted involvement of the participants in the creative process. Those involved expressed surprise at the end result, saying it was very different to what they had expected.

Individual Development and Personal Relationships

Seeing a play is a shared, communal experience. To read a lecture is, of necessity, more abstract in nature—we engage with the written word rather than a human being, although study groups can, of course mitigate this. Steiner keenly felt the need to supplement his lectures and writings with participation in other art forms. Of the drama, he stressed its ability to explore the spiritual development of a single individual—in this case, Johannes Thomasius—whereas *Knowledge of the Higher Worlds* is, of necessity, a general guide for everyone and thus inevitably more abstract in character:

> Should one actually describe the path of development as seen in the spiritual world, one can do it only by shaping the development of a single human being, by altering for the individual what is necessarily true. The book, *Knowledge of the Higher Worlds*, contains, to a certain extent, the beginning of the secrets of all human development. The Rosicrucian Mystery contains the secrets of the individual, Johannes Thomasius.[9]

It is indeed this personal quality which gives the drama its resonance. If, for example, one reads in a lecture that in the astral world people can appear aged differently to how they are in the physical world, such an idea, such an intellectual construct, may quickly disappear, making a swift exit from one's consciousness. Why not? We do not live in the astral world; we live in the physical world. To muse pleasantly over such a notion whilst reading the book—perhaps even to discuss it in a study group—may easily result in its disappearance when we go out into the street and have the traffic to worry about.

The very sight of two characters on a stage who have *visibly* changed age—as happens to Capesius and Strader in scene four, etches such an image deeply into the inner recesses of our minds and souls. It is arresting. It is far more likely to stay with us.

Another related aspect to this matter of the personal quality of drama is its ability to focus on personal relationships. One will search high and low in any of the basic anthroposophical books for an examination of such matters. In Steiner's time such intimate interactions were not publicly discussed in the way they, perhaps rather incessantly, are now. The character of the romantic, Romantic artist, Johannes Thomasius, allows Steiner more latitude in this domain.

The intimacies of Johannes throughout the dramas—especially the first and the third—alert us to the wiles of Lucifer, the Lord of Desire. They reflect much that pertains to contemporary life. The relationships of all the characters afford us greater understanding of the workings of reincarnation and karma. The strange effect of the fairy stories of Felicia Balde upon the learned scholar Capesius indicates the presence of a karmic bond between these two totally dissimilar characters.

Similarly Theodora's revelations affect Strader. This, the first play to seriously examine the question of previous incarnations, allows us to enter into this subject in a fully human way. Lectures are, of course, necessary and helpful, but characters on a stage can convey aspects of the topic unavailable to the spoken or written word alone.

The rich input on this subject accounts partly for the length of the drama. The fairy-tale plot could easily have been wrapped up in the first seven scenes. The individuality of the characters is, however, allowed to blossom in the second half of the play. The metamorphosis of the Maya Temple of scene five into the Sun Temple of scene eleven is, in fact, aided by the development of the characters and the felt need for them to help and support one another. This must be established as their karma requires.

The repeated words of Benedictus in scene three:

> There forms itself
> within this circle
> a knot out of the threads
> which karma spins in world becoming.[10]

are integral to the plot of this play and a fundamental theme running through the four dramas. They run as a harmonious counterpoint to the fairy-tale plot. The awakening of humanity to an understanding of reincarnation and karma was a central task in the mission of Rudolf Steiner. The concerns of the fairy tale—building the bridge uniting the spiritual and physical worlds—needed to be augmented with reference to reincarnation and karma. Johannes and Maria are shown to be united when Theodora reveals their previous Hibernian incarnation. Such revelations are necessary in our own time and were later supplemented by Steiner's lecture series on 'Karmic Relationships'.

The Light

In so many ways the motif of 'the light' plays into this drama—one can say that it is a drama of the word and a drama of the light. It seems fitting to end this chapter where the play itself ends—with Theodora's declaration to Strader:

> 'I have now conquered for myself
> the power to reach the light.'
> My friend trust in yourself!
> For you yourself will speak these words
> when once your time shall be fulfilled.[11]

The final words of the drama bring us full circle from the very first two lines in which the children in Sophia's room are singing:

> The light of the sun is flooding
> the realms of space.[12]

This motif of 'light' constantly interweaves throughout the play. The dark depths of scene two, the horror of scene three, the thunder of scene four and the dangers of scene ten are always mitigated by the light of wisdom. In the shape of Benedictus it is never far away and the motif continues with the prayer he gives Maria's child:

> The heavenly powers of light are carrying me
> into the spirit's house.[13]

The light-filled wisdom of Benedictus grants us the wonderful mantra of scene three:

> Light's weaving essence radiates
> through far-flung spaces
> to fill the world with life.[14]

Which changes in scene seven:

> Light's weaving essence radiates
> from man to man
> to fill the world with truth.[15]

The darkness of scene two changes for Johannes in scene nine:

> There lives in me the light,
> there speaks around me brightness,
> there germinates in me the light of soul,
> there works in me world radiance.[16]

The final scene in the Sun Temple sees the light truly flooding in. References to light abound.

A cryptic contrast emanates from Felix:

> It was men's very folly that from dark depths
> has shown me to the light
> and let me find my way into the temple.[17]

The Maria forces are united. The Beautiful Lily, who harmed those she sought to help through the blinding force of righteous light, needed the warmth of love from The Other Maria.

The Other Maria declares:

> My feeling shall in future
> not rob the light of love of its effect.[18]

As Johannes is the central character, one can conclude with Luna's joyous declaration to him:

> You may then dare to live yourself as Self
> when light can shine within your soul.[19]

and in a superb culmination uniting the development of the individual and the ending of the Tale, we see that Johannes also requires the sacrifice of The Other Maria:

> The sacrifice you bring the temple
> shall here be re-enacted in my soul.
> In me the warmth of love shall sacrifice
> itself unto the light of love.[20]

The Birth of the Portal—A Modern Mystery Drama

'This Play must not be placed in the same
category as those of Shakespeare or the
"Faust" of Goethe.
It is a fresh development in Art.'

Harry Collison.[1]

A familiar shibboleth of spiritual seekers is the love of terms of entice-
ment such as: mystery, esoteric, secret, hidden, occult and veiled.
The joy of uncovering something unknown to others has indeed pri-
mordial appeal. When we hear the term, 'Mystery Drama', it is easy
and tempting to envisage a theatrical production with some esoteric
content to excite the palate. Theatrical producers, fairground managers, writers of pulp-fiction page turners have all happily employed
that term, 'mystery'.

The use of the term for Steiner's Mystery Dramas stems from
far richer and more profound origins—those of the ancient Mystery
Schools whose purpose was the spiritual development of the neo-
phyte and resulting enrichment of society. Those of Ancient Greece
bestowed upon us the genre of tragedy.[2] As Clifford Leech remarks:

> For the Greeks, tragedy was a rite in honour of the presiding
> god, Dionysus, whose priests were present in reserved seats,
> like canons in a cathedral.[3]

The Greek tragedies were purposed to bring about a process of pur-
gation, which Aristotle referred to as 'catharsis'. During the play
the emotions of pity and fear are aroused in the audience—pity for
the turmoil and suffering of the hero and fear for his fate. The end
of the play, with the death of the hero, leading to the cleansing of
the malaise in the society brought about by the hero's weakness or
indiscretion (his tragic flaw) purges the audience of these emotions.
A contemporary Mystery Drama involves, instead, a process of
cognition—but one which must also etch into the souls of the audience. Like the tragedies of the Greeks it engages all aspects of the
psyche—not simply the intellect; still less that of emotional pathos.

The Greek plays honoured the god Dionysus. In a Dionysian rite, three tragedies would be followed by a satyr play (a semi-romantic drama of gods and heroes), to calm and reassure the audience. To achieve an effect of similar proportions but appropriate to a contemporary audience, plays of considerable length are required. In Steiner's dramas the calming effect occurs throughout the play. At the end of each scene we have to be able to calmly assess the situation.

Whilst it is not necessary for a guide to Steiner's *The Portal of Initiation*, to go deeply into theatrical history, it is helpful for us to understand that the play, paradoxically, is part of a genre that dates back to time immemorial, yet it is also a radical innovation, opening a portal into possibilities previously undreamt of. As Collison says, 'It is a fresh development in art.'[4]

The point of connectivity with the Greek tragedies is the effect on the souls of the audience. One can trace a path through from Greece and Rome to the Elizabethans and especially the tragedies of Shakespeare. He explored every aspect of that genre with heroes ranging from the purity of Romeo and Juliet, and Hamlet to the dastardly villainy of Richard the Third. His last four plays moved away from tragedy and ended happily. Did he have a subconscious wish to write a contemporary Mystery Drama? If so—it would have been impossible. The word 'heresy' was on everyone's lips at that time. *The Tempest*, in all its genius, was as far as he could allow himself to venture into esoteric realms.

It was that great admirer of Shakespeare, Johann Wolfgang von Goethe a century and a half later in Weimar where he had both Roman Catholic and Lutheran friends and heretic hunters were absent, who was able to write the modern Mystery Drama: *Faust*. The connections with *Faust* in terms of the length and spiritual content are obvious, but as Collison remarked, *The Portal of Initiation* is essentially a new beginning.

The Fairy Tale

The fairy tale, as Steiner describes,[5] opened new vistas on his work on Goethe. It was in 1883, when Steiner was only 22 years old that he became the editor of Goethe's scientific writings for the *Deutsche Nationalliteratur*. He cites 1889 as the 'germinal point of this drama'(i.e. *The Portal of Initiation*).[6] It took a period of 21 years of gestation—he states that it takes seven years for, 'the seeds ... to descend; then they return, and for this they need seven more years'.[7] He says of the fairy tale:

> This 'riddle fairy tale' has had many interpreters. I was not at all interested in the 'interpretation' of its content. I wished simply to accept this in its poetic, artistic form. I had always an antipathy against the dissipating of creative fantasy through intellectual interpretation.[8]

The last sentence indicates why this spiritual teacher needed to use all the art forms available to him to counter academicism—the mere development of the intellect.

So the drama has, as well as roots in Mystery Dramas, the fairy tale as its seed. In the nineteenth century and early part of the twentieth there was considerable interest in fairy stories and folk tales. They were seen in many European countries as part of a national heritage that had to be cherished. In Germany the Brothers Grimm, whose careers spanned the end of the eighteenth and first half of the nineteenth century, collected the tales and generated much interest therein.

Internationally, musicians, writers and artists delved into the Aladdin's cave of songs, stories and legends of their own countries as rich sources of inspiration. In Steiner's own time, W.B. Yeats, for example, reaped such benefits and, prior to his encounter with abstraction, Wassily Kandinsky along with the other artists Steiner worked with in Munich tapped into this source. Whilst women like Felicia Balde, living on lonely mountainsides and telling their own tales were few and far between, scholars of such sources were less uncommon.

Goethe's tale, as well as having roots in the stories told him by his mother, which fired his imagination as a child, is an alchemical allegory originating in his extensive knowledge of and studies into this cosmic realm—hence its potency and its resonance for Steiner.

The Plays of Edouard Schuré

To conclude this brief sketch of some of the salient influences on the play, it would seem amiss not to mention the dramas of Edouard Schuré, a long-standing friend of Rudolf and Marie Steiner.

Marie Steiner translated works of Schuré including his influential best seller, *The Great Initiates*, and several plays. The pivotal Munich Conference of the Theosophical Society featured Schuré's, *The Sacred Drama of Eleusis*, which neatly takes us back to where this account started, the Mystery Schools of Ancient Greece. It features the mysteries of Persephone. Schuré's plays have featured strongly in the anthroposophical society ever since. Richard Ramsbotham actually cites Schuré as the prototype of Johannes Thomasius in a fascinating article in *New View* magazine.[9] One could also speculate that if Schuré is the prototype, perhaps Goethe himself also plays into the character as, like the polymath of Weimar, Johannes Thomasius becomes both artist and scientist in future plays.

Realism and Spiritual Realism

The discussions between Sophia and Estella in the Prelude and Interlude mirror the disputes of the time both in the theatrical world and the realms of art and literature between the advocates of realism and the champions of symbolism. In France, the Théâtre Libre of André Antoine attempted to show 'life as it really is', eschewing theatrical conventions and employing 'realist' writers such as Emile Zola. The Théâtre Libre (1887-1896) was highly successful in influencing theatre companies in France and further afield in Europe, particularly the Independent Theatre in London and the Freie Bühne in Berlin.

The Symbolists advocated poetic theatre, not the 'prose' of mundane reality. Amongst the foremost theatre directors in France were Paul Fort whose productions in the Théâtre d'Art were influential but short-lived (1890-92) and the more widely influential Aurélien Lugné-Poe, who worked in Antoine's Théâtre Libre initially but became convinced that the intangible elements of spirituality, dreams and visions were the true essence of human life. His Théâtre de l'Oeuvre (1893-1929) introduced the plays of Strindberg and Ibsen to French audiences. Symbolism in the visual arts, poetry and the theatre was influential throughout Europe.

The discussions between Estella and Sophia in the Prelude and Interlude were thus a reflection of the disputes of critics and theatre-goers at this time internationally. The realist writers, as Sophia indicates were novelists and dramatists of quality such as Zola, Ibsen, Chekhov and Strindberg. The debate now seems to have been won by the realists whose contemporary efforts consist of soap operas, disaster movies, bio-pics and reality shows. That discussion seems even more relevant today than it was when the play was written.

Steiner's spiritual realism remedies the deficiencies of the realist dramatists, who may seek to leave us with 'tear-stained faces', but ignore the spiritual world. It also ensures against any tendencies to idle fantasy that may encroach on symbolist productions. Such radicalism as we encounter in the Mystery Dramas remains challenging even for contemporary audiences. The enrichment afforded by these plays does, however, ensure that the rewards are truly life-changing.

The Scenes

The Prelude and Interlude form the framework of the play. Scenes one and eight both mirror and elevate the arguments in the Prelude and Interlude. The first seven scenes, with the addition of the final scene reflect the plot of the fairy tale, especially from scene four onward. The symmetry of the scenes is both deliberate and complex. The first scene, with all the characters is naturally reflected in the concluding scene, but also parallels scene eight as a foundation for the ascent of the language. Scene two is antecedent to scene nine, scene three thrusts us into scene seven, scenes four, five and six deliver the nexus of the fairy tale. Lucifer and Ahriman can be traced from scene one through to scenes three, four and ten.

Each individual scene has a level of self-containment greater than that which tends to be the case in conventional drama. This is because the audience must relax at the end of the scene. Often in theatrical productions we find ourselves sitting anxiously awaiting what happens next, when the curtain dramatically descends. This cannot be so in the Mystery Drama. We engage with the characters, but need to calmly assess their situation rather than to have our emotions shaken up on their behalf. This ensures that each scene begins and ends in a state of calmness and therefore has a kind of completion within itself. The individual scenes thus have a quality of readability clearly intended by the playwright. Such lavish productions as the Mystery Dramas clearly limit the possible number of actual performances, however they do well facilitate both individual and group readings and study sessions. This was demonstrated by Steiner himself in lectures featuring scenes from the dramas.

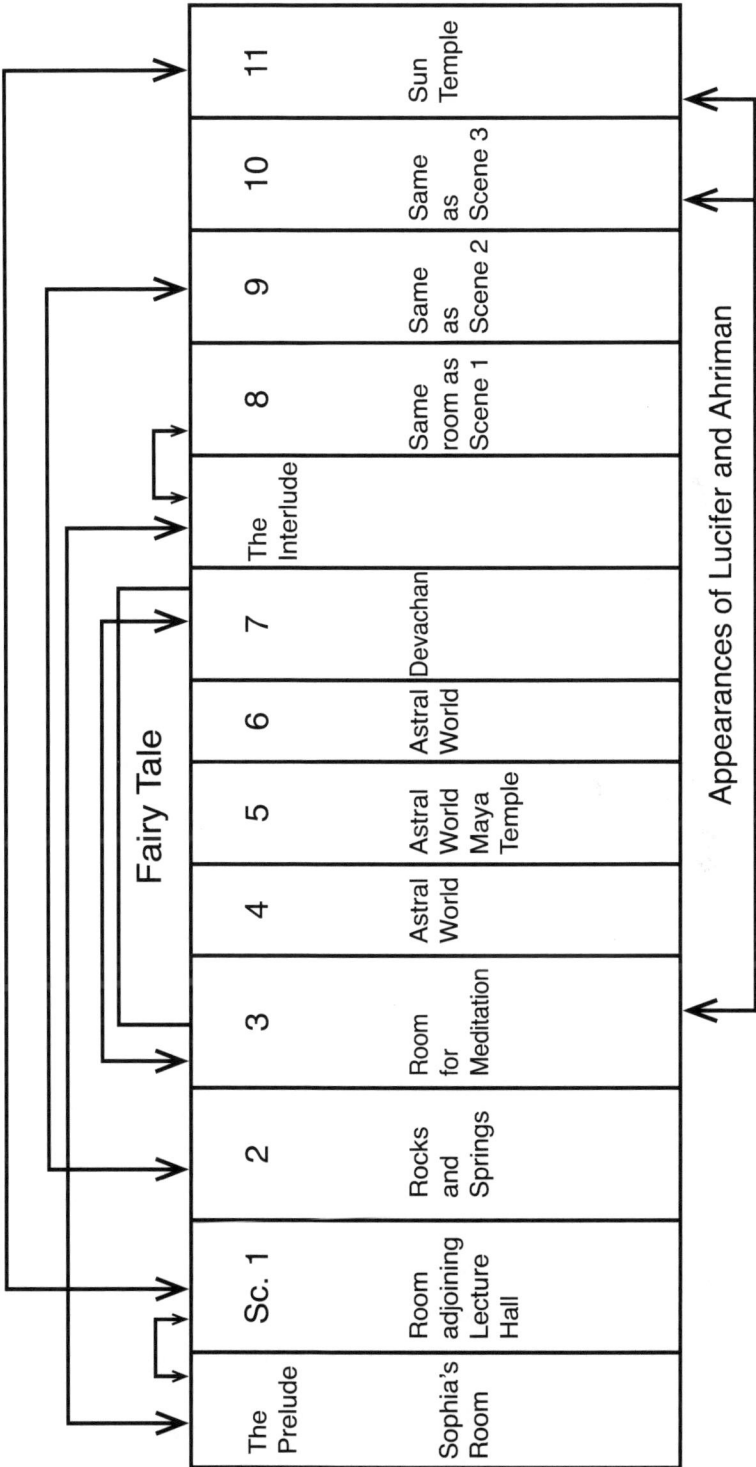

The Prelude	Sc. 1	2	3	4	5	6	7	The Interlude	8	9	10	11
Sophia's Room	Room adjoining Lecture Hall	Rocks and Springs	Room for Meditation	Astral World	Astral World Maya Temple	Astral World	Astral Devachan		Same room as Scene 1	Same as Scene 2	Same as Scene 3	Sun Temple

Fairy Tale

Appearances of Lucifer and Ahriman

The Prelude

Just as the Greek tragedies often included a 'chorus', who would forewarn the audience and set the mood for the play, so Rudolf Steiner skilfully and poetically situates the 'Prelude' and the 'Interlude' within the structure of *The Portal of Initiation*. They are as essential to the play as the overture is to Mozart's *Magic Flute*.

The mood of the audience is immediately lifted with the song of the children accompanied by Sophia on the piano. The appropriately simple words delightfully embody the Goethean spirit of the drama and the underlying theme of spiritual unity.

The entry of Estella precedes the first of many Socratic-style dialogues throughout the play, posing serious questions to the audience. These allow us to ponder freely our own responses whilst we listen. The dialogue between the anthroposophist, Sophia and the sceptical, vivacious Estella is of central importance to both those already committed to the anthroposophical path and those hovering near it. Why? The reason is, as Hans Pusch[1] points out—we all have something of both Estella and Sophia within us. He poses the questions:

> Is Estella not fully justified? How much of what Sophia says sounds more idealistic than real?

Those familiar with the writings of Steiner often remark on how he, as an initiate, is able to immerse himself in the viewpoint of opponents whose ideas are at variance with his own. The publication of his book, *Friedrich Nietzsche, Fighter for Freedom*, occasioned some to perceive him as a follower of the author of *The Anti-Christ*. Similarly in the discussion with Sophia, Estella is awarded some extremely hard-hitting lines which should surely cause some soul-searching amongst anthroposophists.

In response to Estella's inquiry, Sophia informs us that her husband is attending a conference of psychologists and hoping to speak. He is, however, sure that his views will be poorly received. This prefigures the theme in the final drama of the difficulty of bringing spiritual science into society. The positivistic notions of Capesius and Strader pose such obstacles in the present play.

Estella proposes that they go to watch a play whose title translates as either, *Outcasts from Body and Soul* (Collison) or *The Uprooted* (Pusch). It clashes, however, with a performance of a play by Sophia's society. In the following discussion, Estella expresses her anxiety:

> But your world
> of ideas—which is so alien to me—will destroy
> even the last remnant of our friendship that has
> bound us together since our schooldays.[2]

This is a common problem for those who become spiritual seekers. Friendships formed prior to them embarking on a spiritual path, with those now sceptical of such ideas, are less easy to sustain than they otherwise would have been. Sophia and Estella admirably retain their mutual regard in spite of their contrasting outlooks.

A debate then commences about their different ways of looking at life. Estella hits hard:

> But actually the direction of your ideas
> makes you assume a certain superiority ...
> Your view, however,
> claims to be more profound than all the rest, which
> it looks on simply as products of a lower level of
> human development.[3]

Is there no truth in such accusations? Is it not likely that the playwright is drawing attention to such flaws in his followers?

She continues with more hurtful body punches:

> Just think of those of your friends
> who try to impress with the mere pretence of
>   profundity!
> ... those fellow-thinkers who swear
> by your ideas and display their spiritual
>   arrogance

> in the worst possible way … and I won't remind
> you how callous and unfeeling some of your
> adherents have been towards their fellow men.[4]

Such words are clearly not lacking an element of truth and demand that the audience sits up and takes note. It has to sadly be admitted that the subsequent history of the anthroposophical society bears out Estella's accusations. Steiner is warning his followers against these tendencies.

The conversation moves on to a discussion about art. Estella is sophisticated and sensitive. She responds to realism in drama and literature. It should be remembered that the realists of Steiner's time included dramatists and writers as notable as Chekhov, Strindberg, Ibsen and Emile Zola. The discussion of the two protagonists seems even more pertinent now that this genre has since descended into instantly assimilated and equally instantly forgotten 'entertainment'. Sophia is on firm ground. Their discussion helps to inform our understanding of the working of the play.

Estella's accusation that Sophia's 'kind of drama' displays 'puppet-like types, indulging in symbolical events',[5] shows us that the playwright is not only aware of such dangers but is resolutely not going to fall into such a trap. The characters in *The Portal of Initiation* originate in those of Goethe's fairy story, *The Green Snake and the Beautiful Lily*, but certainly take on a life of their own. Ethical individualism was a term he used to describe his philosophy; it would be unthinkable for the characters in his plays to be lacking a certain personal autonomy. Steiner was very clear on this point:

> I can remember something that happened just last year when we were performing Schuré's play, *The Children of Lucifer*. How shocking it was to the dramatist, who is an artist in the best sense of the word, when someone came up to him to ask, 'Does this character represent Atma, this one Buddhi, a third Manes, or maybe this one is Kama Manas?' etc., etc. This kind of allegorizing is simply impossible in a truly creative, artistic process, and it is just as impossible in an explanation or interpretation. Therefore, it can be said that no one should be

pondering the anthroposophical meaning of Johannes Thomasius. To this question there is only one answer: as the main character in the drama, he is nothing more than Johannes Thomasius. He is nothing more than the living figure, Johannes Thomasius, in whom nothing more is portrayed than the mystery of development of one man, Johannes Thomasius.[6]

Sophia answers Estella by referring to the 'living creative spirit that forms human beings with the same elemental power as the germinating forces in Nature form a seed'. Estella has only an intellectual notion of the spirit as being an instrument of knowledge. Thus her idea of what art should be is divorced from the spiritual.

The two protagonists reappear in the Interlude and on each occasion resolve to remain friends.

Scene One

'When many people join in conversation,
their words present themselves before the soul
as if among them stood mysteriously
the archetype of Man.'

Maria[1]

Composition, Themes and Structure

The first scene, not only of this play, but of all the four plays, which have to be viewed as single entities, but also as a unity, introduces us to all the major characters. It is a lengthy scene—the longest in the play—and much information is imparted to the audience about the characters. A commercial director would avoid such an 'overload', but Steiner's purpose is the presentation of a Mystery Drama, which will work in the manner described by Sophia in the Prelude, where she insists that:

> As little as the forces of the seed have to teach the plant to grow but rather unfold within it as a living entity—so little do our ideas teach. They pour themselves into our being, life-enkindling, life-bestowing.[2]

Such growth can only occur at its own pace. The scene does, however, proceed quite rapidly from the introduction of one character to another.

The scene is finely structured, both within itself and in relation to the whole play. It begins and ends with the conversations between Johannes and Maria, like the aperitif and the dessert course, followed by the delightful vignette of Johannes and Helena providing the double espresso with the silver paper-wrapped mint chocolate.

By the time the scene concludes, we have not only been introduced to all the characters but we have heard them as a totality. The idea that we each tend to be rooted in one of the twelve world views, so that the 16 characters can collectively be seen as a single entity, encompassing them all, is finely alluded to in Maria's speech:

> When many people join in conversation,
> their words present themselves before the soul

as if among them stood, mysteriously,
the Archetype of Man.[3]

Twelve is a number suggesting fixity and completion, as with the twelve zodiacal constellations. Similarly seven is a number of movement and completion as with the seven major planets. This also applies to the seven colours of the rainbow, as Maria continues:

It shows itself diversified in many souls,
just as the pure light, the One,
reveals itself within the rainbow's arch
in many-coloured hues.

Johannes has to experience this totality as preparation for the difficult, but necessary Kamaloka experience of scene two. By the end of the conversation, he has experienced:

A mirrored image of the whole of life
that showed me clearly to myself.
What is revealed to us out of the spirit
has led me to perceive how many men,
who think themselves a whole, in fact
bear in themselves one single facet only.[4]

The idea of the twelve different viewpoints is explored throughout the dramas, particularly in *The Soul's Probation* and *The Guardian of the Threshold*. In this scene there are more than twelve characters, but the totality is expressed.

The need was to experience such a variety of standpoints, and compressing them into one scene gives the audience a stronger feel for the turmoil they experience at the end of it than would be the case had the scene been divided. The discomfort was needed by both actor and audience! The only other scene with so many characters is the final scene—the opening and the closing of the curtain of the play.

The feeling of the Prelude is recaptured in the dialogue between Capesius and Strader (the Will o' Wisps in Goethe's tale) and the followers of Benedictus. This argument on the merits of the spiritual scientific standpoint and those of positivism is expanded and now related to personal experiences.

We glimpse the different unities and karmic relationships between the characters: Johannes and Maria; Maria, Philia, Astrid and Luna; Capesius and Strader; Capesius and Felicia Balde; Strader and Theodora and Luna; Felix and Felicia; Felix and Benedictus—and the totality of them all. The theme of karma is fully introduced in scene three, but the groundwork starts in the first scene.

Many other themes are introduced, or else further extended from the Prelude: Theodora's vision of the Etheric Christ is a keynote to all four plays. We also encounter: spiritual science versus positivism, the development of Johannes, faith versus cognition, and the acceptance of diverse individualities (i.e. Theodora and Felix). Evil, in the form of the bust of Ahriman and the gushing of Helena prepare us from the beginning of the play, for the stage debuts of Lucifer and Ahriman in scene four.

The Action

The first speech of Maria conveys the strength and depth of her love for Johannes. She tells of how her heart felt his pain and how she shared his dreams. The strength of their relationship and the nature of it is a strong strand which runs through the plays. The brief dialogue between them at the beginning of this scene shows the brooding self-absorption of Johannes—here, much the romantic artist—contrasting with the compassionate, altruistic nature of Maria whose principal concern is to help others. She is The Beautiful Lily of the fairy tale; Johannes is the, initially disconsolate, Prince.

Just as the Prince is accidentally wounded by the Lily, Johannes finds that Maria's attempts to help him as an artist:

> robbed me of the interplay
> of my soul forces.[5]

In spite of, or because of, her own development, she is unable to help others.

Her difficulties occasion the first appearance of Philia, Astrid and Luna, the 'Handmaidens of Lily' in the tale, who are, at times, representative of the soul forces of an individual, but also, elsewhere, of the universal, cosmic forces. Philia's remarks about how there were, in the meeting, harmonious tones, but also a harsher dissonance, are made whilst Strader and Capesius come on stage. The timing of entrances and exits often carries such implicit resonance.

Entry of the Wisps

Capesius and Strader have their fairy-tale origins in the two Will o' the Wisps who rock the Ferryman's boat and refuse to pay their fare. They represent those karmic forces of change which are often disruptive. Capesius as a historian, pondering 'the changing character of different epochs'[6], has been relatively successful and managed to impart some enthusiasm to his students, but has come to the conclusion that human thought-life is a dry and shadowy affair. He has found in the group a lack of dogma and feels, to an extent, drawn to its teaching, but, 'cannot quite surrender to it yet'.[7] He is battling with himself.

Strader is more vigorously sceptical, warning that such revelations as those expounded by the group may be heart-warming, but, for a thinker, they are mere wishful dreams. Philia's reply points out that materialistic science does not satisfy the feeling realm. Strader knows this to be true, but tells of how he battled through his cloistered youth to the belief that spiritual teaching was a misty dream and that positivistic science brought clarity. This battle in his youth shows us Strader has strong will forces and a seeker's yearning for clarity of thinking that he has been unable to find. In this discussion, the soul forces (Philia and Luna) are those of Strader. Although Luna argues against the coldness of Strader's ideas, the conflict is within Strader himself—as demonstrated by his very presence in this company, which indicates a yearning for spiritual nourishment in spite of his scepticism.

It is significant that while Luna is speaking, Theodora—who will decisively help Strader's progress—appears. Luna, who embodies the will force has a strong affinity with both Theodora and Strader. The karmic revelations of Theodora are will-imbued.

Divergence

At this point the Wisps diverge; we see a marked difference in the two sceptics, Capesius and Strader. The former impatiently dismisses Maria's description of Theodora's clairvoyance—which has something of the old atavistic nature—whereas Strader regards it in the way that a scientist with an open mind might regard an unexplained phenomenon. He wants to see Theodora experience a revelation. Her pivotal account of Christ in the etheric impacts strongly on Strader. The scepticism of Capesius is well portrayed. He argues that Theodora is a conscious or unconscious victim of auto-suggestion, having heard about the Etheric Christ from the teacher, Benedictus.

The two Wisps share the same frustrations of having a dried out, materialistic way of looking at life, but whilst Strader is Aristotelian in character and looks outward to the world for evidence in forming his views, Capesius is more of a Platonist, whose tendency is to brood and look inward. Whilst the experience of Theodora's revelation shocks and moves Strader, it is the fairy stories of Felicia which have an enlivening effect on Capesius. This duality is fruitful in that persons of opposite natures can form powerful alliances. As the dramas progress, this is proven threefold with Capesius and Strader, Capesius and Felicia and Strader and Theodora.

The Woman with the Basket and the Man with the Lamp

The entry of Felix and Felicia Balde marks a change of mood away from the argument between the Wisps and the believers. They bring a different atmosphere with them. As country folk influenced by nature spirits they have a strong affinity with the fairy tale, in which Felicia is 'The Woman with a Basket' and Felix, the wise 'Man with the Lamp'.

Capesius perks up and momentarily stops being a Wisp. He becomes a gentleman. When Maria asks Felicia if Capesius visits her, he gallantly jumps in:

> Assuredly, and I must truly say
> I owe to this good lady
> my deepest gratitude.
> She gives me of her gifts so richly,
> as no one else can do.[8]

After his fulsome praise of Felicia, however, when the Baldes have left, wispiness and ridicule return. We learn of Capesius's inability to understand the nature wisdom of Felix at this juncture:

> He speaks of sun-born beings
> that dwell within the stones,
> of moon-dark demons
> who constantly disturb this work,
> about the sense of number in the plants.
> A listener will not for long
> find any meaning in his words.[9]

One can well imagine the ridicule of contemporary media upon the utterances of the nature-wise Felix. Benedictus has already told Felix that each word of his has infinite value and he gently rounds on Capesius the mocker:

> But one can also feel
> as if strong powers of nature sought within
> his words to manifest themselves in their own
> being's truth.[10]

Doubt

The exit of Benedictus, following that of Felix and Felicia, marks a further change of mood.

Strader feels so stirred by Theodora's vision that he relates how a subconscious force causes him great discomfort by challenging his way of thinking:

> But oftentimes when unsolved riddles torture me,
> there rises ghostlike to my spirit vision
> a frightful, dream-born being out of spirit darkness.
> It lies upon my soul like lead
> and, terrifying, clutches at my heart.
> It speaks through me:
> 'You must compel me
> with your stunted weapons of dull thought,

> or you are nothing but
> a fleeting phantom of your delusion.'[11]

The language here is arresting in its vigour. 'Unsolved riddles', do not usually 'torture' people. The last four lines are repeated with effect by The Spirit of the Elements in scene four. Gone is the Will O' Wisp. Here we are jolted by the honesty and openness of Strader's fear of doubt. The references to 'spirit vision' and 'spirit darkness' make us question the quality of his apparent materialism.

The first sentence of Theodosius's reply is pertinent:

> This is the fate of those
> who can only approach the world through thinking.[12]

The rest of the well-meant speech from the erstwhile 'Spirit of Love', however, denies the possibility of cognition in spiritual matters and has the saccharine quality of the utterances of some modern clergymen. It only stimulates Strader to revert to a Wispy short-shrift:

> The fruit of pious faith
> is able to bring peace to souls
> who can, sufficient in themselves,
> seek out such ways.

Reliance on 'pious faith' has been deeply unsatisfying to him. He concludes with a lofty put down:

> But strength of real knowledge
> will never thrive on this path.[13]

The entry of The Other Maria, whose archetype is The Soul of Love, and the presence of Theodosius, inspired through The Spirit of Love, bring a quality of soul-warmth. The Other Maria corresponds to the Green Snake in the fairy tale. The mannerisms of the Snake, who happily devours the gold coins of the Wisps (representing wisdom in this case) are adeptly transmuted into those of The Other Maria:

> The warmth and magic power of words
> that here I listen to,
> streams down into my hands

and flows through them
like balsam, when they touch the sorrow-laden;
and it transforms itself upon my lips
to strengthening words which carry comfort
 to pain-racked hearts.
I do not ask the source of these words' power.[14]

The sensuous delight she derives from these altruistic deeds is masterfully depicted.

Capesius then argues that good works may be done by those who do not listen to spiritual teachings.

This stimulates the lengthy exposition of Maria, in which she forwards ideas corresponding to those of Sophia and concluding the argument in a similarly skilful and authoritative manner. She tells the Wisps:

Though clear and sure may seem
your thinking, that lives in the old way,
it can supply the tree's dry bark
but does not reach
into the living power of the heart.[15]

The following conversation between Romanus, Capesius and Gairman puts questions in our mind. The enigmatic nature of both Romanus and Gairman is a worthy subject upon which to ponder. When we later encounter the former as the embodiment of The Spirit of Action and the latter as the vehicle for The Spirit of the Earth Brain, it is difficult to marry this with the seemingly rather superficial individuals chatting before us[16].

Gairman is the Giant in the fairy tale and Romanus the Bronze King. The potential of each human being is particularly underlined in the case of Romanus—the analogy of the seed and the tree, which recurs in the speeches of Maria, the representative of the Christ force, is brought before us in compelling guises. The wilful individual who enjoys the 'whirr of wheels' may bear the seed of future greatness. Gairman's frivolity sardonically references the dilettante who enjoys playing with spiritual ideas—but even he has been stirred a little by the lecture, or so he says.

Further Changes of Mood

The denouement of the scene is the dramatic revelation of Johannes to Maria of the terrifying effect that the lecture and the conversations have had on him—the realization of the fatal effect of his leaving:

> A gentle human being,
> who once had linked her destiny
> with mine in faithful love.[17]

followed by his victory over Lucifer, in the form of Helena. Maria, whose own inability to help causes her distress (as with the isolation of The Beautiful Lily in the tale), knows that they must seek the help of Benedictus.

The interchange between the seductive Helena and Johannes lightens the mood and warms the hearts of the audience, showing us that with all his failings, Johannes can bring himself to be strong. The chidings of Helena are a quite commonplace idea that spiritual seeking is a happy, clappy comfort zone. Johannes ends the scene on a note of triumph:

> But that words of highest wisdom
> are only an illusion of the soul in *you*,
> a single moment has revealed.[18]

The audience is left feeling relaxed and slightly amused, waiting and wondering how the dilemmas of Johannes, Maria, Strader and Capesius will play out. To leave us simply with the tension and anxiety of Johannes's anguish would have been counter to the ideals of the Mystery Drama. The rules of conventional drama tell us that is how it should end—the principles of 'spiritual realism' state otherwise, allowing us breathing space.

Scene Two

'The world and my own nature
are living in the words:
O man, know thou thyself!'
Johannes.[1]

It is with some trepidation that one takes on the task of writing about this truly iconic scene. The scene itself is something of a play within a play. Prior to the entry of Maria, it takes the form of a tumultuous poem in free verse. The rhythmic quality of the language interspersed with the strong resounding repetitions of the call to knowledge—handed down to us from the Ancient Greek Mystery Schools—imbues the drama with a resonance which etches into the souls of the audience.

It is essential to understand that what we are seeing—and hearing—are the storms raging through the consciousness of Johannes during the first scene. Whilst 'flashbacks' are not uncommon devices in films and dramas, this portrayal of the soul processes is unique to the Mystery Drama.

'O Man, Know Thou Thyself'
Johannes has meditated often on these powerful mantric words. '*Erkenne dich*', translates literally as, 'know yourself', however whilst the German has a strong consonant cluster, the English is very vowelly and needs the added strength of the alliteration afforded by, 'O man, know thou thyself'. The archaism is deliberate—'thou' and 'thyself', were archaic at the time Collison, Bittleston and Pusch were translating. It adds to the memorable quality and rhythmic resonance of the mantra.

The scene itself has its counterpoint in scene nine in the second half of the play, during which the emphasis switches from the fairy tale to the individual development of the characters. The seed of that process is planted in the first scene and its initial sprouting is in this scene, in which Johannes's soul is laid bare. The Prince of the tale, a necessary but subsidiary character to the Lily and the Snake, becomes the central character of the play. The principal focus is upon his development—so memorably shown to us in this scene.

The narrative is the Kamaloka experience of Johannes as he experiences the pain of the woman he deserted. He thought little of it at the time; she died of a broken heart. He then has the horrific encounter with his lower self, described in, *Knowledge of the Higher Worlds* as the meeting with the Lesser Guardian of the Threshold. Spiritual Realism arrives in tooth and claw.

These are wholly realistic experiences within the dramatic framework. We can take comfort from the fact that Rudolf Steiner explained that most people do not have the experience of suffering the anguish they have caused to another during their earthly life. This takes place in the spirit world after death. Only an initiate, or one striving towards initiation who is sufficiently prepared, will experience such events during earthly life. Whilst one should certainly not be fearful of such matters—Johannes remains composed throughout—it is also telling that the scene occurs immediately after Helena's narcissistic babblings of 'blissful freedom' and 'joy of spirit'. Spiritual progress inevitably entails strife.

Structure and Content

The dramatic poem which comprises the first six speeches takes us into the soul world of Johannes Thomasius. The landscape itself is a projection of his soul and echoes his exhortation to himself: 'O man, know thou thyself'. The nature imagery continues throughout the play. The soul of Johannes enacts a kind of breathing process. He has to become free of his own physical body, and then return to it. Movement resonates during these six speeches, or stanzas. The mood changes throughout the process; we see a fluency of movement in the poem itself.

The Journey Begins

The first stanza is an expression of wonder. Wonder has to be experienced by the seeker. Without the feeling of veneration, progress is not possible. Johannes compares the power of the mantric words to the acorn in which:

> secretly
> the structure of the mighty oak is pressed.[2]

The growth of the seed was previously referenced by both Sophia and Maria. It is a powerful metaphor, reverberating through the drama. Spiritual science itself is a seed with such potential.

Fear and Alarm
The following stanza sees a complete mood change. The imagery is of 'darkness', 'blackness' and 'soul-blackness'. Johannes's initial statement:

> And now!—within me
> it is becoming terribly alive.[3]

shows that he realizes—and warns us, the audience—that there is no turning back. He must engage with the experience. To overcome fear is necessary at this juncture; a strengthening of the ego is required for further spiritual undertakings. The ability to stand firm and hold one's nerve is even more pertinent in spiritual development, in which one can easily lose one's bearings, than is the case in day-to-day life.

Kamaloka
The third rendering of the call to knowledge augurs the Kamaloka experience itself. We watch, spellbound as Johannes loses himself— and takes us with him. The imagery is stark as he melts into the universe, becoming one with the cosmos:

> And now it robs me of myself,
> I change with every hour of the day.
> I melt into the night.
> The earth I follow in his cosmic course
> I rumble in the thunder,
> I flash within the lightning,
> I am—[4]

We move into the realm of what a psychiatrist might term a 'psychotic episode'. The list of involuntary actions: 'I change', 'I melt', 'I follow', 'I rumble', 'I flash', fire up in quick succession; they end with the simple 'I am'. Our own imaginative faculties are jolted as we journey into the cosmos with him.

The whole landscape is the soul of Johannes. He now becomes separated from his physical body:

> I see my body's shell.
> It is an alien being outside myself;[5]

Johannes is not stricken with the horror of the experience. We can see why such a situation can only be experienced by someone who is able and ready to deal with an encounter of this nature. He, like the audience, is able to view the event with detachment, whilst experiencing the trauma. We are wholly removed from film or theatrical conventions, which would doubtless depict tears and angst. The fact that he can commentate lucidly on the situation shows an element of calmness and self-possession on his part.

He experiences that which is normally endured after death—the suffering of one to whom we have done harm. Through her mouth he *has* to speak. He *must* 'suffer her despair'. He understands and reassures us that:

> Self-knowledge lent me strength
> to pour myself into another self.[6]

We feel privileged to share this difficult experience with Johannes— giving us an insight, adding another dimension to that afforded by lectures. The unresolved karma of his chequered past appears in later dramas as 'The Spirit of Johannes Youth', a burden he is tasked to carry.

The Lesser Guardian

The following three sections, or stanzas, describe Johannes's encounter with his lower self. This is described in *Knowledge of the Higher Worlds*, as the meeting with the Lesser Guardian of the Threshold. It would horrify and disorientate one who was not sufficiently prepared for it.

We are fortunate in having excellent translations of the Mystery Dramas by Harry Collison, Adam Bittleston and Ruth and Hans Pusch. Throughout this book I have used the Pusch translation as it is still in print, unlike those of Collison and Bittleston. For this section, I will quote from Collison. His version captures well the visceral quality of Johannes's encounter with his lower self. He refers to them as:

> Experiences of the lower human nature expressed in emotion, will and thought and described as bestial.[7]

Johannes informs us of these horrors:

> Like some fierce dragon do I see myself;
> Begotten out of primal lust and greed.[8]

The unveiling of the sludge of one's lower ego is a shock:

> Some dim deluding veil of phantom forms
> Hath hid from me mine own monstrosity.
> Mine own self's fierceness must devour my Self
> And through my veins run like consuming fire
> Those words, that once with elemental force
> Revealed the core of suns and earths to me.[9]

The imagery of this section is savage—'fierce dragon', 'devour', 'fierceness', 'monstrosity', and the words of the mantra, 'throb within my pulse' and 'beat within my heart'. A relentless torrent of self-flagellation continues through these three sections. We feel the pain that Johannes bears, knowing that we all have our 'own monstrosity', but Johannes maintains a level of self-possession and we learn from his travails. We could not do so if moved to tears ourselves.

In the following section the imagery is of servitude: 'chains', 'riveted', 'forged' and 'chained'. Naturally it is unnerving when he asks the dreadful question:

> So fast was not Prometheus riveted
> Upon the naked rocks of Caucasus,
> As I am riveted and forged to thee—
> Who art thou, fearful, execrable shape?[10]

At this climactic moment the call and the echo resound, 'Know thou thyself, O man.'

It is Johannes himself—his lower self! Johannes's reaction suggests he is not too surprised:

> Oh yea, I know thee; for thou art myself:[11]

He realizes his former blindness:

> And now once more within thy sightless soul
> Blind through these words: 'Know thou thyself,
> O man.[12]

It is interesting to compare the different translations. Collison likes to use iambic pentameter, and these few examples from his translation, I hope, give a flavour of his work. I shall now revert to Pusch.

Reassurance

We have been taken to the limits with the drama of the scene. We have to be brought down before the scene ends—calmness must reign, nerves must not jangle.

> Maria, you are here![13]

is the prosaic greeting as the bringer of reassurance enters upon the erstwhile tumult. This is as it should be. Maria is the calming presence who will guide both Johannes and the audience into less stormy waters. She has instinctively sought out Johannes, although she cannot help him. She knows that solitude has been precious for him as an artist. Solitude, which can involve a kind of narcissistic brooding as well as tranquillity, is clearly no longer the pleasure it once was after these shattering experiences.

Johannes describes to Maria what he has gone through. She, like the Beautiful Lily of Goethe, is haplessly helpless to assist him, but knows that only Benedictus can help them both. The language is much less heightened and the audience is afforded its mandatory state of calm at the climax of any Mystery Drama scene. The strength of Maria's feeling for Johannes is further revealed as is her steadfast faith in the spirit:

> You must live through each terror
> to which illusion can give birth
> before the truth reveals itself to you
> thus speaks your star.
> Yet through this starry world is also clear to me
> that we must wander on the spirit paths together.[14]

The scene, however, would not be complete without a further reminder of the call to knowledge. The rhythmic repetitions demand the closure of a further echoing. Johannes reminds us of his suffering:

> They force me out of fear into the darkness,
> and hunt me through the darkness into fear,
> these words imbued with wisdom:
> O man, know thou thyself!'
>
> (*From the springs and rocks resounds:*)
> O man, know thou thyself.[15]

Scene Three

'There forms itself within this circle
a knot out of the threads
which karma spins in world becoming.'[1]

A central core of the mission of Rudolf Steiner was that of bringing into being an understanding of the processes of reincarnation and karma. The eight volumes of the lectures on karmic relationships and the four Mystery Dramas were the primary vehicles affording an explanation of this theme in relation to specific individuals. It is only through the study of the sequential lives of specific individuals in different eras that the workings of reincarnation and karma can be understood—not just intellectually, but in a truly holistic way.

The lectures give us case studies of real lives; the dramas show fictional characters, of whom Steiner insisted that there was nothing of a fanciful or made-up nature. Everything in the drama is, in a heightened sense of the phrase, rooted in reality.

A Quiet Beginning

Scene three introduces the audience to this theme and contains what Eileen Hutchins describes as, 'one of the most difficult passages in the whole series of plays'.[2] The initial dialogue, between Benedictus and Maria, begins serenely, creating a feeling of calmness within the audience. The words of Benedictus for the nourishment of the soul of the child:

> The heavenly powers of light are carrying me
> into the spirit's house.[3]

resonate with those in the Prelude, which commences with the children singing:

> The light of the sun is flooding
> the realms of space.[4]

The imagery of light and darkness weaves through the entirety of the play.

The Pertinent Question

Maria requires Benedictus to advise her as to why her attempts to help others are counter-productive. The child left on her doorstep prospers and thrives when she nurtures it (the child can be either gender. Bittleston has it as a girl, as does Collison. In the Pusch translation, it is a boy.) When, however, the child begins to love her, its gifts decline.

Maria is calm, even somewhat matter-of-fact, showing emotion only briefly when describing how:

> His young heart stirs warmly
> whenever he looks lovingly at me.[5]

She simply asks the necessary question, demanding an answer:

> Do not deny my asking this grave question:
> why do I ruin friend and child
> when lovingly I try to do for them
> the work that spirit guidance
> lets me perceive within my heart as good?[6]

The Karmic Knot

Benedictus has quietly allowed Maria to take control and manage the conversation up to this point. He now takes over, with a lengthy explanation of the complex situation. He comes straight to the point:

> There forms itself within this circle
> a knot out of the threads
> which karma spins in world becoming.[7]

The karmic knot of the successive, interweaving lives of the characters begins to unravel in this play, but it is not until the fourth drama, showing us the incarnation of the characters in Ancient Egypt, that the karmic revelations conclude.

The Answer to the Question: a Special Task

Benedictus then affords us a charming and, from an anthroposophical standpoint, delightful description of Maria's character, karmic
past and upbringing. Everything occurs at the right time—she is not
greedy for things she is not ready for; things have happened as they
should, in accordance with nature and spirit:

> Your course of life had fitted you
> as mediator of new healing forces.
> In many lives you had acquired
> an openness for the nobility
> alive in human hearts.
> The precious quality of beauty,
> the highest claim of virtue,
> you carried in your gentle soul
> as spirit heritage.[8]

The spiritual world required Benedictus to find someone with the
wherewithal for a very special task:

> There came to me a higher being
> which should descend into the realm of earth
> to take up its abode within a human body.[9]

A human being fit to become such a spirit vehicle had to be found.
Such an experience could only occur at, 'a turning point in time'—
an essential juncture in human destiny. Maria is one who has the
innocence and purity, not of naivety, but of maturity. She, the Beautiful Lily, was the obvious choice for such a vital role.

The Mechanics of this Process

Essentially, the destiny of Maria is that of bearing the spiritual consciousness appropriate to the Michaelic era in which the atavistic
clairvoyance has to be replaced by informed cognition.The Archangel Michael needs to work through Maria. Rudolf Steiner explains
how at such pivotal moments in human evolution the interweaving
of the spirit being and the human is essential:

To understand how someone like Abraham could make such an important contribution to human evolution, we must keep in mind an important truth: whenever a person is chosen to meet a specific function in human evolution, direct intervention by a spiritual being is required.

He goes on to describe how in this scene of *The Portal of Initiation*:

The hierophant makes Maria aware that before she can fulfil her mission she must be influenced by a higher being. Consequently the higher members of her body separate from the lower and are possessed by a subordinate spirit. If you allow this scene to work on your soul, you can begin to see great mysteries in human evolution.[10]

This extraordinary scene surely merits such a claim.

The conditions suffered by Maria, whereby she has a stultifying effect on those who she wishes to help are uniquely her own individual experience at this turning point of time:

> The spirit in you works
> in everything that can grow ripe in man
> as fruit for realms eternal.
> And therefore much it must destroy
> that only has its place on the realm of time.[11]

The problems caused by the purity of Maria's spirit having negative effects on the child and Johannes are temporary and will be transcended:

> What flourishes for higher life
> must bloom from death of lower being.[12]

As Collison explains:

The higher ego in Maria is building up the Spirit Self. The power of the Spirit Self in Maria destroys what is not yet purified in other souls—but it stimulates them to spiritual development.[13]

Maria is so shocked by the revelation of her having been chosen for this mighty task that:

> Her soul is soaring forth to spirit heights.[14]

Just as Capesius and Strader need shocks for their development, a pupil of Maria's level has also to undergo such experiences.

Johannes

The presence of Benedictus guides Johannes through a nightmarish experience as 'the enemy of good' (Lucifer)[15] enters Maria's physical body, which then becomes 'a gruesome being'[16], vitriolically abusing Benedictus. Johannes has managed to refrain from panic and stay reasonably calm, retaining his faith in Benedictus, despite the accusations against their teacher, seemingly emanating from Maria.

The final speech of Benedictus is lengthy, beginning with his explanation to Johannes of the invasion of Maria's physical body. The references to the spirit that perpetrated this action gradually escalate from, 'the enemy of good', to 'an adversary', 'the tempter', and finally, 'the prince of hell'.[17] We are being prepared for the appearance of Lucifer and Ahriman in the following scene.

Benedictus reiterates to Johannes the words he spoke to Maria:

> There forms itself
> within this circle
> a knot out of the threads
> which karma spins in world becoming.[18]

He reassures Johannes about his progress and promises future success:

> My son you have stood firm so far,
> you will progress still further.[19]

Forces have to unfold in the spirit seeker which are not founded simply on the requirements from day-to-day living. The striving Johannes has endured has prepared him for future development:

> You are now found mature
> You now may be released.

Your friend has led the way.
In spirit you will find her.[20]

A Serene Ending

Benedictus promises further help and then gives Johannes a mantram for his spiritual journey. The imagery is of love and light. Collison urges that we should study this and that the words:

> should be learnt in German for cosmic forces are contained
> in the very sounds of these words. They are 'redeemed
> words'.[21]

So the scene ends with truly mantric words, followed by a prayer
from Benedictus beginning:

> O spirits who can be perceived by man,
> quicken with life the soul of this our son.[22]

This prayer receives acceptance from the spirit world and is mov-
ingly responded to by the Spirit Voice reiterating the sentiments
expressed in the first scene about the insubstantial nature of earthly
thinking:

> thoughts now guide him
> to depths of world-beginnings;
> what as shadows he has felt
> soars out beyond the world of forms—
> world, of whose fullness
> men, when thinking,
> dream in shadows;
> world from whose fullness
> men, when seeing,
> live within phantoms.[23]

The Spirit Voice functions in a similar way to that of the Chorus
in the Greek tragedies. Our appetite is whetted for the following
scene and the encounter with Ahriman and Lucifer, also our mood is
warmed and lightened after Maria's apparent transformation into, 'a
gruesome being'.[24]

This arresting scene is beautifully balanced so that, once more, we do not get entangled in the horror of the arrival of the forces of evil, and a situation which to medical science would seem to belong in the psychiatric ward. The scene begins with the calm authority of Maria and ends with the avuncular descriptions and advice calmly given to Johannes by Benedictus—whose presence is always reassuring—followed by the Spirit Voice. It makes strong demands on the actors—especially Maria. Her spirit has left the body, which thus loses mobility, whilst her shrill outpouring of vitriol must have the grandeur of a powerful spirit entity.

Scenes four, five and six move more into the realm of the fairy tale and we wait in suspense until scene seven to find out the fate of Maria. Johannes's presence is retained—the actor has to work continuously.

Scene Four

'Two powers stand before the world of soul.
The one dwells in us as tempter;
the other dulls the gaze
when it is turned toward outward things.'[1]

Johannes

The Stage Debut of Ahriman and Lucifer

It was a historic occasion when Ahriman and Lucifer first appeared on stage in Munich in 1910. The part of Lucifer is often played by a female actor, and 'has golden hair' and 'wears crimson robes'. Ahriman, 'the conventional Satan, wears yellow robes.'[2] The previous binary conception of good/evil, God/Devil, having outlived its usefulness, is replaced in Steiner's cosmology by the Trinitarian configuration of Christ holding in balance the forces of Ahriman, who attempts to fix humanity's gaze to the material world, and Lucifer, the Lord of Desire, who tempts us to the ecstatic realms of worldly neglect.

It is beyond the scope of the present text to further explore the theology,[3] but it is certainly pertinent to draw the reader's attention to Steiner's understanding that simply describing this radical interpretation of 'evil' in lectures, although necessary, was not enough to afford a full, experiential and cognitive grasp of these 'necessary powers of hindrance'. The sculpture, *The Representative of Humanity*, fixes an unforgettable image of them being held in balance into the memory and psyche of the viewer. Mantras demonstrating the viewpoints of Lucifer, Christ and Ahriman help to imprint an understanding into our soul faculties. The depiction of them onstage affords us an imagery upon which our creative forces can set to work. The theatrical demonstration of the way in which the two powers collaborate deepens our comprehension of much that occurs in life.

In scene one, the bust of Ahriman is present from the beginning and the scene concludes with Lucifer speaking through the seductive lips of Helena. Throughout the drama the Christ forces are shown through the dialogue and actions of Maria and Benedictus. The brevity of the initial appearance of the two forces of adversity helps to endow it with a memorable quality—they come and go quickly but we can never forget them. Each briefly describes their history and their perception of their tasks.

Lucifer has often been played by a female; s/he is tempter and beguiler. Each of the two parts has to be fine-tuned; movements and voices have to be convincing. The part of Ahriman is particularly challenging, with his steely coldness—although not so much in this brief appearance in which he is competing with Lucifer to charm and lure Johannes. Throughout the dramas the pair work together as it suits them, but there is a less emphasized element of competition between them. Here Ahriman uncharacteristically refers to 'beauty', as both are tempting Johannes, the artist:

> I could shine out for you
> with pride of beauty,
> with bliss of revelation.[4]

One would normally associate the last two lines with the temptations of Lucifer, who brought to us the realm of art.

Another noteworthy aspect of their speeches is the mixture of truth and falsehood. A recurring motif throughout the four plays is the fact that the adversarial powers will speak the truth whenever it suits their purpose so to do. Lucifer speaks truly when stating that he gave us, 'your own will'.[5] To achieve freedom, Adam and Eve had to eat the apple, as Lucifer, through the serpent, tempted them. Lucifer, however, created the lower self of the human being, which Johannes recognizes, but is yet to overcome.

The inversion of the lines introducing and concluding their initial speeches is significant:

> *Lucifer:* 'O man, know yourself.' *Ahriman:* 'O man, know me.'
> 'O man, experience me.' 'O man, experience yourself.'[6]

They are, at this stage of human development, a necessary counter-point to one another. Their redemption can only come about when humanity reaches higher levels of maturity and redeems itself.

It is important to note that this scene is experienced by Johannes in meditation. Lucifer and Ahriman do not feature in the fairy tale;

the play differs from the tale in regard to its focus on the individual development of Johannes Thomasius, who, in this brief encounter, triumphs by recognizing them, occasioning their exit. The following events in the scene follow closely the events of the story and the atmosphere changes, moving in the direction of the charm of the fairy tale.

The Elemental World

We are still viewing the meditation of Johannes. The 'Spirit of the Elements' appears with Capesius and Strader, 'whom he has brought to the earth's surface from the earth's depths. They are conceived as souls looking out upon the earth's surface.'[7] Collison further informs us that, 'the Spirit of the Elements is aged and stands upon a sphere'. The Wisps are 'in astral garb'. Capesius wears blue robes of various shades; Strader wears brown and yellow.[8] The scene has an arresting visual quality.

The Spirit of the Elements is the Ferryman in the tale. This part of the fourth scene and the following two scenes have a close relationship to the tale. The Ferryman can take passengers across from the land of the spirit to the material world. The equivalent in Greek mythology is Charon, who ferries passengers across the River Styx; he is also the Lord of the nature spirits.

Just as the Wisps jovially and boisterously rocked the Ferryman's boat, Capesius and Strader have caused problems to the Spirit of the Elements:

> The spirits and the elements
> arose in raging storm,
> when I was forced to enter
> their kingdom with your beings.
> Your kind of thought resisted
> the ruling of my power.[9]

The Spirit of the Elements is the guide to incarnating souls when they enter earthly life and accompanies sleepers returning to their etheric and physical bodies.

In this vision of the astral world, Capesius, who in earthly life is in his mid-fifties and Strader, who is in his early thirties, are seen as being aged differently. Capesius appears to Johannes as being younger, bouncier and more idealistic than his earthly counterpart; Strader is depicted as elderly, cantankerous and cynical. They are Wisps par excellence.

The depiction of Strader (a young man) as elderly and Capesius (in his fifties) as young, is challenging for the actors; it is, perhaps, even more so for members of the audience. Steiner explains[10] that in the astral world our ordinary concept of time is not applicable; it is fully realistic to depict Johannes's vision of Strader and Capesius in the astral world, as being of different ages to those of their physical bodies. Time, in the physical world, is of the nature of a semblance or maya. It is only in the context of the material world that, 'time waits for no one'. This is one of those anthroposophical concepts that is not difficult to grasp intellectually, but to fully internalize such a proposal on all levels requires meditative work. This depiction onstage of the inverted ages of these characters opens our doors of perception:

> When we look into the astral world, it is first of all necessary to overcome the primary maya of the sense world in order to understand the power of time… It is not that time is stretched forward and backward but that one man is shown in his youth, the other in his old age. It is an absolutely real fact.[11]

The dialogue which began in scene one, with the Gentlemen of the Wisp expressing dissident views to the spiritual seekers is, in a sense, continued in scene four. Their expressions of materialistic reasoning and their pride in their educated thought elicit the replies of the lightning and thunder—clearly indicating their disharmony within the elemental world.

It is difficult to believe that what we think, or even what we say sometimes, has serious repercussions. Johannes is graphically shown that such is the case. Capesius is initially full of youthful idealism, also vanity:

> I sense the whole world's might
> within the beating of my pulse.
> Anticipation of all I shall achieve
> is rising in my heart….
> (*Lightning and thunder from the heights and depths*)[12]

The Spirit of the Elements penetrates the veneer of Strader's scepticism. He makes inroads—Strader's apparent certainty is painfully pierced:

> *Spirit of the Elements:*
> Then it behoves you to acknowledge
> that no man can know
> from whence are gushing the sources of his
> thought
> or where life's first foundations lie.
>
> *Strader:*
> O these words, they are the same
> which in my youthful days of hope
> resounded terribly
> within my soul,
> when all support of human thought,
> believed so firm, began to sway.
> (*Lightning and thunder*)
>
> *Spirit of the Elements:*
> You must compel me
> with your stunted weapons of dull thought,
> or you are nothing but
> a fleeting phantom of your own delusion.
>
> *Strader:*
> Once more such terrifying words …[13]

They echo his own words in scene one, showing the fragility of his hitherto apparent certainty of self-composure. He retains his defiance, but Capesius is left to deal with the Spirit.

In keeping with the scene at the beginning of the tale where the Wisps pay the Ferryman in gold, which rocks the boat and could pollute the river, Strader and Capesius refuse to pay The Spirit of the Elements in the required manner. Just as The Woman with the Basket has to pay three onions, three cabbages and three artichokes for the debt incurred to the Ferryman by the Wisps,

Felicia is saddled with that of Capesius and Strader to the Spirit of the Elements. Gifts bestowed by the spirit necessitate repayment; as she has bestowed her tales on them, she has to pay their debt.

Contrasts

When the Spirit of the Elements departs, we see in the brief dialogue between Capesius and Strader, prior to the entrance of The Other Maria, the Aristotelian, outgoing nature of Strader and the inward looking, Platonist nature of Capesius. On the departure of the Spirit, they have to decide how to proceed. Capesius suggests they should:

> … obey courageously
> the impulse of our inner selves.
> To me this impulse says:
> Let truth become your guide …[14]

Looking inwards will be the most productive way forward. Strader contrarily proposes looking outward:

> The man who serves none but himself
> need follow only his heart's urge,
> but he who wishes to help others
> must know for sure
> just what his life requires.[15]

Enter: The Other Maria

The mood changes with the entrance of The Other Maria. The stage directions in Collison[16] tell us: '(The Other Maria, also in soul-form, emerges from the rocks, covered with precious stones.)' Strader alerts those of us who simply read the play that The Other Maria's appearance has a fascination—a kind of aura:

> But look—what a mysterious being!
> It is as if the rock itself
> had given birth to it,[16]

Strader retains some of his haughtiness, but is influenced by The Other Maria, without wishing to admit it. His last two speeches in this scene are dismissive:

> You cannot help us then …[17]

And

> That is no way for us.[18]

But that initial exclamation, 'What a mysterious being…' and his now becoming more of a listener, show that she has some effect on him—not the drastic effect of the seeress, but that of a difficult-to-explain phenomenon, not capable of being tamed by the intellect. Capesius is similarly, but more visibly, 'taken' by The Other Maria. Her connectivity with the natural world relates to his hunger for the fairy tales of Felicia:

> *The Other Maria:*
> I wrest my way through rocky depths
> and seek to clothe the rock's own will
> with human words;
> I sense the being of the earth
> and wish to think the earth's own thoughts
> within the human head;
> I drink in air of purest life
> and bring the powers of air
> transformed to human feeling.[19]

Capesius then tells her:

> I love your language, woman
> and gladly would translate your kind of speech
> into my own.[20]

The speeches of The Other Maria are always preceded by music— Steiner gave Adolf Arenson, the musical director a particular melody, often played on a lyre or flute. In the Foundation Stone Meditation,

Rudolf Steiner distinguishes between, 'simple shepherds' hearts' and 'the wise heads of kings'. The Other Maria resolutely belongs to the shepherds' stream. She radiates the warmth of love. She is a nurturing and loving person, unable to conceptualize spiritual science, as her counterpart, Maria, is able to do, but she can absorb it just as the Green Snake in Goethe's tale swallows gold coins (symbols of wisdom).

The fairy tale is mirrored when The Other Maria informs them that the Beautiful Lily (Maria):

> Dwells within the realms
> From which you have just come.[21]

The Wisps in the tale also made the wrong crossing when hoping to find the Lily and like them, Capesius and Strader are unsure how to proceed. In the tale, the Wisps had the option of crossing the river at noon with the Snake—consciously and in full view of everyone. The other method was by using the shadow of the Giant at dusk, suggesting atavistic clairvoyance and the lowering of consciousness. The Other Maria seems to indicate a choice of a kind of Goetheanism on the one hand:

> If you will give your souls
> to all the pure delights of my existence,
> you will soar forth on spirit wings
> toward primal origins of worlds.[22]

Alternatively they must:

> Forget what reason must dictate.
> Let Nature's mood first conquer you.
> In manhood's breast let childhood's soul,
> untouched by shadow—images of thought,
> hold sway, naively true.[23]

Eileen Hutchins suggests that the first method is that of the Gospel of Saint Matthew and the second, that of Saint Luke. It is clear that

neither way suggested by The Other Maria is the way of cognition—
that of fully imbibing spiritual science. In the tale, one can clearly
see that the crossing at noon with the Snake represents the path of
conscious devotion and self-sacrifice (that of the Snake herself), or
the unconscious path of the old clairvoyance, or hypnotism, trance,
narcotics etc. (the vacuity of the Giant). Capesius concludes that
they need to work and wait patiently; the ways suggested are not
suitable for modern scholars. The scene concludes with Johannes
recalling his meditation.

Scene Five

'But now in human souls we shall do fruitful work
united with the Brothers
who serve the Temple's work of consecration.'[1]

The Other Maria

'As long as on earth
only those men gain a hearing
who have no wish to call to mind
their spirit's origin,—
so long the beings mighty in the ores
in depths of earth will hunger.'[2]

Felix Balde

Retardus

Romanus   +   Benedictus

Theodosius

The quotations for this scene are taken from Adam Bittleston's translation, to give the reader a flavour of his work. It has a pleasing clarity whilst retaining much of the poetic resonance of the original.

This scene would have been a revelation to its initial audience, with its four altars and their hierophants giving an atmosphere of an uncovering of secret rites. It retains its visual impact. To bring that wisdom which had hitherto remained strictly guarded by secret societies into the public domain—a wisdom whose time had come—was a task central to the mission of Rudolf Steiner. It is the theme of this scene. There is a strong correspondence with the underground temple scene in Goethe's tale, in which the temple later moves to the surface from its hidden location.

This brotherhood poses challenges to the actors; it is only Benedictus who is fully present. Collison describes Theodosius and Romanus as 'etheric haloes', so there needs to be a degree of unworldliness in their speech—this has to be finely tuned and not 'overdone'. Coupled with the strong visual impact, the unusual quality of the voices of the participants and their unique personas imbue it with a memorable resonance.

A contrast with the fairy tale is, again, the focus on the character of Johannes. Benedictus can help Johannes, but needs the co-operation of the other hierophants.

> I showed him Light, which led him
> to the first spirit seeing. If for him
> what is now picture should grow to truth
> your work must join with mine.
> My word proceeds from me alone;
> through you World Spirits sound.[3]

Johannes is able to picture aspects of the spirit world, but is unsure as to the truth of his visions. He needs to know whether they are simply his artistic imagination, or reality itself.

We have encountered Theodosius and Romanus as members of Benedictus's audience in scene one. Now we see them in their robes. Benedictus himself is arrayed in gold, white and red; in the fairy tale he corresponds to the Golden King. It is Theodosius whose resplendent apparel of silver and blue who corresponds to the Silver King and Romanus in bronze and green, who completes the regal triumvirate as does the Bronze King in the tale. They respectively embody the forces of thinking, feeling and willing. The Mixed King of Goethe is a retarding force who ludicrously falls to pieces and whose defeat signifies progress. Retardus is similarly reactionary and similarly defeated.

The temple itself is situated in the astral world, into which Johannes is able to see. Benedictus wants to help him to advance further—perhaps eventually being able to pass The Guardian of the Threshold and to become an initiate. The astral world is, one could say, an intermediate world between the Earth and the Spirit world of Devachan. It contains an element of illusion—there streams into it truth from the Spirit World, but also falsehood from luciferic spirits. Steiner refers to the temple in scene five as, 'a Maya Temple', a 'Fata Morgana'.[4]

Steiner explained that to consecrate the working together of the forces of spiritual powers within a human individuality, in the temple, human representatives of the individual forces of wisdom (thinking), love(feeling) and action (willing) had to work in unity. The persona certainly seems to incorporate a paradoxical element. Romanus, in particular, when we saw him in ordinary life, came across as a mundane, not particularly perceptive individual. Now we see him as a hierophant! The Oxford English Dictionary definition of 'hierophant' is:

> 'a person, especially a priest, who interprets sacred mysteries or esoteric principles'.

Clearly this suggests an element of gravitas seemingly lacking in Theodosius and, especially, Romanus. Steiner explained the apparent incongruity by indicating that, 'the primal forces of will'[5] can work through such a person as Romanus. As an analogy, one can look upon Benedictus as a fully fledged flower and Romanus as a seed which has the future potential to blossom. His energy and drive imbue him with a great potential, if he develops the forces of cognition.

It is important for us to understand that Johannes's development requires him to see the astral temple as 'reality intermingled with maya':[6]

> In Scene Five a maya, a Fata Morgana of the spiritual world is pictured, from which, after it has been experienced, the soul must free itself.[7]

Theodosius, like Romanus is a complex character. Romanus's archetype is the Spirit of Action—he is not a man interested in spiritual matters; the working of a dynamo or the sweat of human endeavour are the prime fascinations for him. Theodosius has the Spirit of Love as his archetype—not, however, pure, Christ-like love. Sentimentality, sensual love, egotistical love—that which engages the warmth of the feeling realm is his field of advocacy. We later see how he is prone to the influence of Lucifer.

We can see the distinction between Benedictus, whose whole spiritual constitution is in balance and who is fully present, and the 'etheric haloes' of Theodosius and Romanus. Benedictus closes his first speech with:

> My word proceeds from me alone:
> through you World-Spirits sound.[8]

In contrast, Theodosius and Romanus respectively begin:

> *Theodosius*: Thus speaks the power of love
> which binds together worlds
> and with real being fills the spirit.[9]

> *Romanus:* My words as well
> do not reveal my separate being:
> there speaks the will of worlds.[10]

Retardus is only shown in the play as a spiritual being—one artic-
ulating the wiles of Ahriman. There had been debate in occult
societies as to whether esoteric ideas should be brought into the
public domain as Blavatsky and the Theosophists had done. There
was considerable resistance and Steiner still endured more of such
opposition. Steiner described Retardus as 'the Ahriman of necessity', as previously it had been necessary to oppose luciferic forces
leading to spiritual bliss and earthly disregard. A turning point
in time had come, however, when the defeat of Retardus became
imperative.

Retardus can be seen as representing reactionary forces—his
thinking is shallow and his feelings unbalanced. His will forces
are geared to his own survival. If we met him as an individual,
he would be something of a nostalgic bore. One could understand the caution of those occultists who wanted to keep the
secrets to themselves—the experiment of spiritualism had not
been a success. The time, however, had arrived when change
was required.

The configuration of the altars bears a symbolic element. Retardus is in the frozen North—Ahriman is an ice-cold spirit. Romanus's
presence in the West suggests the non-contemplative action-thought
of Western society (at the time the play was written, the Futurist art
movement with its love of action, racing cars and technology, was
nearing its heyday). Benedictus is the truly progressive force, here
situated in the East. Theodosius, whose emphasis is in the feeling
realm, is in the sensuous warmth of the South.

In this scene, witnessed by Johannes in his meditation, Theodosius
speaks well and impresses both Johannes and the audience. Later he

becomes a mask for Lucifer, but his response here to Benedictus tells
how Johannes:

> … draws near the spirit of the world
> through offering up the illusion
> of his own separate being.[11]

Theodosius offers the warmth which will:

> awaken the spirit
> from his soul's being.

Johannes's soul must grow firm for him to see what happens in the
spirit world:

> And love will give him power
> to feel himself as spirit
> and so create for him the ear
> that hears the words of spirit beings.[12]

Through Theodosius, the Spirit of Love inspires Johannes to put
aside his lower self and develop his spiritual vision and ability to
hear the Spirit World. Romanus then calls upon the spirits of the
hierarchies to creative activity:

The aims of spirits who shape worlds	(Archangels)
will quicken him.	
The spirits of the first beginnings	(Archai)
will fill his spirit.	
World Powers will	(Exusai)
grant strength to him.	
The Mights of spheres	(Dynamis)
illumine him	
and Lords of worlds	(Kyriotetes)
shall give him fire.[13]	

Retardus is confident, at this stage in the proceedings that he can hold back the enthusiasm and thwart the intentions of the others:

> The earth has not made known to us
> in any way a wish for new initiates.
> Until some men, who uninitiate,
> can yet find spirit through the things of sense,
> enter the space in which we meet—
> I am allowed to check your zeal.[14]

The other hierophants need the presence of ordinary people who have not been initiated, but who wish for the wisdom of the temple. Whilst such a request is left unuttered, Retardus can maintain control:

> I hold back your spirit light
> within this Temple, that it bring not
> harm instead of soundness,
> meeting with souls who are still inactive.[15]

This heralds the dramatic and decisive entry of Felix Balde and The Other Maria. The mood changes again, as Romanus, the mouthpiece of the Spirit of Action rounds on Retardus:

> Since the beginning of the earth
> we had to suffer you among us.
> But now the time allotted for your work
> has run its course.[16]

Their entry is pivotal and it is the speech of Felix that forms the centrepiece of the scene. Having heard Capesius's dry remarks in scene one, dismissing Felix's 'eccentric speech', we now witness just how sharp an observer he actually is. He has loved the solitude of his mountains, but now:

> A power which speaks to my spirit
> out of the depths of earth, has bidden me
> to go into this place of consecration.[17]

Just as the entry of the Man with a Lamp, and the Green Snake into the Subterranean Temple is a turning point in the fairy tale, that of Felix and The Other Maria is decisive in the play. His speech has the wisdom of the Man with the Lamp and has a wickedly ironic energy, as he compares the modern scientist with a merchant wanting to make money from mist! How pertinent to our time is:

> What grows these days in human brains
> can serve the surface of the earth—
> it does not reach the depths.[18]

Greta Thunberg could scarcely have expressed it more succinctly! The scene now moves swiftly through to its triumphant conclusion. It is Theodosius, the Spirit of Love who is the hierophant who at this juncture is interacting with Felix and The Other Maria. He asks Felix the burning question:

> What should be done
> to give the powers of earth
> what they so much need?[19]

The reply is clear, concise and pertinent:

> As long as on the earth
> only those men gain a hearing
> who have no wish to call to mind
> their spirit's origin,—
> so long the beings mighty in the ores
> in depths of earth will hunger.[20]

Just as the altruism of the Green Snake and the wisdom of the Man with the Lamp combine perfectly in the tale, the configuration of Felix, the bearer of the Spirit of Nature and The Other Maria, the Soul of Love, harmonize with charm and eloquence in this scene; she tells him:

> In you the spirits of the earth arose,
> creating light for you apart from science.

> In me a love could work, that of itself,
> develops in existence among men.
> But now in human souls we shall do fruitful work,
> united with the Brothers
> who serve the Temple's work of consecration.[21]

Benedictus, Theodosius and Romanus urge Felix and Maria to unite with them so that, 'initiation will achieve its work'.[22] Retardus, rather pitifully, asks, 'What will become of me?'[23]. Benedictus replies with generosity:

> You will transform yourself
> finding a new existence
> because your work is done.[24]

The reply of Theodosius:

> In sacrifice you will live on
> if you will sacrifice yourself.[25]

serves to focus our attention not only on the defeat of Retardus, but upon the eventual fate of 'the necessary powers of hindrance', Ahriman and Lucifer. Eventually if humanity attains sufficient maturity, they too will be redeemed and as Romanus tells Retardus:

> You will bear the fruit in human deeds
> if I can cultivate these fruits.[26]

Johannes now sums up the action, reiterating what he has seen and calming the mood of triumph. He has been shown how Felix, the other erstwhile lover of solitude, has realized the need to bring his wisdom to the temple, rather than enjoying solitary musings. A powerful bond has formed of the hierophants, Felix and The Other Maria, with the defeat of Retardus.

Scene Six

'What you now give their spirit
is lost to you for your own self;
and loss of vital powers
will show itself in you
as ugliness of body.'
        The Spirit of the Elements.[1]

Scene six has the same setting in the astral or elemental world as scene four—an appropriate setting for Felicia, the teller of folk tales. It similarly follows the action of Goethe's tale, featuring the episode in which the Woman with the Basket has to pay off the debts incurred by the Wisps to the Ferryman. Such a sequence of events seems, to worldly eyes, most unjust. Johannes is again meditating this scene and has to learn that those who help the spiritual development of others must take responsibility for so doing.

The scene divides into three parts: firstly, the dialogue between Felicia and The Spirit of the Elements. This illustrates aspects of Felicia's steadfast character as she accepts the debt. Secondly, we hear the tale itself, providing evidence of Capesius's claims for her storytelling, and finally her dialogue with Gairman—whose archetype is the extraordinary Spirit of the Earth Brain.

The last words of The Spirit of the Elements, spoken to the Wisps, in scene four were:

> It will not do
> that you refuse me payment.
> If you yourselves cannot accomplish it
> then tell the woman
> who has endowed you souls with power
> that she must pay for you.[2]

Felicia is naturally disconcerted at the apparent injustice of having to repay the debt owed by Capesius and Strader simply because she has helped them. The Spirit is not unsympathetic but the rule has to be enforced. Felicia demonstrates firmness and strength of character:

> It's not my custom
> to refuse what I should do.[3]

but flinches understandably when The Spirit of the Elements informs her that the kind, loving help that she has given to Capesius and Strader, invigorating their spirits with her tales—her own life forces—is the reason that her body will now suffer:

> What you now give to their spirit
> is lost to you for your own self;
> and loss of vital powers
> will show itself in you
> as ugliness of body.[4]

The Woman with the Basket in the fairy tale, who had always been proud of her beautiful hands, suffered one of them becoming 'as black as coal', for incurring the debt of the Wisps. The Spirit of the Elements, whose tone to Felicia is kind and sympathetic, comforts her:

> Yet you will work for mankind's good
> and your own happiness as well.
> The mother's beauty and the child's life
> will blossom in a higher form for you
> when one day in the souls of men
> new spirit powers spring to life.[5]

The 'child's life' refers to Felicia's complaint that Strader and Capesius spoilt her son's 'feeling for the spirit'[6] with their materialistic ideas. They meant well, but in fact, did harm. Steiner education is artistic and nourishing to the souls of children. The well-meaning efforts of Strader and the professor cast, 'the dismal shadow of dark science'[7] over Felicia's child who, 'was stricken with soul death'.[8] The reference to 'the dismal shadow' brings to mind the shadow of the Giant in the tale, perhaps forewarning us of Gairman's entry later in the scene.

The task the Spirit sets for Felicia is that of telling a tale to 'inspire the spirits of the rocks'.[9] Felicia's tales follow a natural creative process. She is truly an artist; the tales are organic and not the product of prosaic didacticism. The tale is one that she has told Capesius, but Steiner[10] tells us that she does not know the meaning of it. He instructed Collison,[11] 'not to add any fancy or imagery into it'. Within the tale Felicia expresses the powers of light and heat; her thinking incorporates that of both the intellectual soul and the sentient soul.

Whilst obeying Steiner's instructions—art must never be over-explained—it is pertinent to remind ourselves that Felicia's tale is told to the elemental beings. Although we have seen the disturbances caused in the astral world by 'knowledgeable' utterances of the Wisps, the elemental spirits trapped in the world of sense can be released by enlightened thoughts and feelings, such as those expressed by Felicia. We can imagine she has an eager elemental audience, who would surely be engrossed, and identify with the being:

> That flew from East to West
> following the journey of the sun.[12]

When Felicia tells them that this being observes:

> … how men love one another,
> and how in hate they persecute each other.[13]

these emotions would be puzzling to them. Steiner explains[14] how some elemental beings such as the gnomes have a very sceptical attitude toward human behaviour. Felicia relates how the being continues following the sun without stopping:

> for hate and love create
> always the same a thousandfold.[15]

So it seems an inexplicable, repetitive ritual which simply continues. However, the being espies an old man who has been wrestling with the problem of human love and human hate. It stops with him one night upon its journey. The spirits of the rocks would be curious to see how things work out, however, when the sun returned,

> the being was once more
> caught upward by the spirit of the sun.
> Again it saw the many people
> in love, in hate,
> continue on their earthly course.

This strange human ritual is tantalizing enough to the elementals, but then the story takes a dramatic turn:

> And when it came a second time
> above the house, still following the sun,
> its gaze fell there
> upon the dead old man.[16]

There is no death in the realm of the elemental beings of her audience. The old man has been released from his pondering. Leaving, however, no opportunity for further discussion.

Enter Gairman

The satirical voice of Gairman then resounds sneeringly from behind a cliff. Gairman is an extraordinary creation; his archetype is the Spirit of the Earth Brain. Collison informs us that:

> ... he is especially associated with the seventh stratum of the earth, which reflects in a distorted way the seventh sphere above the earth, the sphere of the prototypes of our moral qualities.[17]

He then quotes Rudolf Steiner as having informed him: 'Its substance changes everything into its opposite'. Collison then adds, 'In the brain of such a man as Germanus[18] are the seeds of revolution.'[19]

He can be seen as the mocking voice of the earth-bound intellect, so aptly dealt with by Felix in the previous scene. We encountered Gairman in the first scene as a man of a rather indolent, frivolous nature, whose thought-life could best be described as easy-going. Now we encounter him as spirit:

> I am the Spirit of the Earth-brain,
>   a dwarf-like copy of me
>   is all that lives in men.[20]

In this scene Collison informs us that, 'Germanus wears brownish robes and is made to appear like a giant with heavy clogs, as if tied to earth.' The three scenes in the astral world provide a fascinating series of visual spectacles.

He is the Giant in the tale—a representative of unconscious processes of spiritual connectivity which now need to be replaced by cognition. His functioning is dictated by habit and caprice. He acts in a half-asleep, impulsive manner, stealing one of each of the vegetables of The Woman with a Basket. (It is important to recognize that when habits are consciously controlled through spiritual development, the forces of the Giant can contribute positively to life.) The vegetables he steals are: an onion, a cabbage and an artichoke—root, leaf and flower. They represent in the arts: the epic, the drama and the lyric.

The power of the Giant's metabolism comes to expression in his shadow; at sunrise and sunset this can be used to cross the river to and from the spiritual world. The inability to do this in daylight—the full light of cognition—represents such practices as trance states, narcotics and other such methods of gate-crashing the spiritual world.

Gairman brings Felicia's story down to earth in more ways than one! The 'Being that flew from East to West', becomes a 'man who tramped from East to West'. He then becomes a 'dry researcher'. Gairman is attracted by the imagery of the traveller and the old man, along with the rhythm of the story. He begins with clarity, trying to parody Felicia's work, substituting a man for the Being, then compressing the old man and the Being into a 'dry researcher' who uses statistics but cannot find a theory to explain the love and hate. He meets two Beings, one of Love and the other of Hate but is deaf to their words. He then tails off and concludes:

> As deaf researcher, he tramped on
> from East to West, this man.[21]

Felicia is hurt by her tale being ridiculed and reduced. She rounds
on Gairman:

> and who are you
> who thus distorts
> each word of mine
> in such uncalled for manner?[22]

Whilst her husband was able to get the better of Retardus, with
the help of some mockery and ridicule of his own, Felicia's task
is harder and she cannot easily dispatch Gairman. She shows that
she is not to be trifled with, but Gairman is allowed the last word.
This is surely symptomatic of our society today. Once again a spot-
light is shone upon the disjointed, spirit-lacking, cynical modes
of contemporary thought processes. In relation to the enigmatic
nature of Felicia's tale, Eileen Hutchins perceptively recommends
pondering upon the meditation given by Benedictus at the close of
the third scene.

Gairman does not make a further appearance in this play. The
Giant in the tale crosses the bridge and is walking to the Temple,
but becomes fixed to the ground like a statue, his shadow pointing
out the hours marked, 'in noble and expressive elements'. We meet
Gairman again in the final two plays, metamorphosed into Magnus
Bellicosus, whose name reminds us of his origin, but who shows a
benevolence and an interest in others—clearly a counterpoint to and
an advance upon his previous persona.

Johannes briefly concludes this scene:

> This was the man who said
> that spirit light had entered
> as of its own accord into his brain.
> And like her husband Felix
> Felicia came
> just as she is in life.[23]

Our sojourn in the astral world is complete. Johannes has been
shown its deceptions and still needs to meet Maria in Devachan to be
sure of the reality of his experiences in the spiritual realms. We can
understand why he still lacks such certainty. The three scenes in the

astral world have furnished the audience with cameos of poetic and visual charm. They add delight to the theatrical experience, but just such qualities encourage Johannes to question their voracity. In this regard, Johannes becomes an Everyman character—we too would surely need reassurance in his position.

Scene Seven

*'Because they show themselves so clearly
in the Devachan scene, everything in it
is alchemy in the purest sense of the word;
all of alchemy is there if one can gradually
discover it.'*

Rudolf Steiner.[1]

This scene is truly the centrepiece of the play—at last we are in Devachan! The first half of the play reaches a grand finale in a setting where the colours are purer and more vivid than in the astral world of the last three scenes. The scenery and the costumes are unsparing of the efforts of the stage designer. Even in translation, the language here, mirroring the splendour of its location is something to treasure—and to work with. Steiner asked Marie Steiner, a uniquely talented vehicle for this work, to demonstrate it in many speech and drama lectures.

It marks the culmination of the fairy tale. Goethe, of course, was well-versed in alchemy, having made a considerable study of the writings of the 'natural philosophers', such as Paracelsus, Jacob Boehme and many others. The fairy tale is in the tradition of the allegories of the alchemists. The play retains much of this alchemical atmosphere, which we experience especially in scene seven, with its references to the ethers, the elemental beings and the aspects of the human soul.

Essentially the scene can be viewed as consisting of three components: it commences with the interaction of Maria, Philia, Astrid and Luna, which concludes with the arrival of Johannes; this is followed by the second revelation of Theodora. Closure arrives to this section of the play with the speeches of Maria to Johannes and Benedictus's blessings to Maria and Johannes, culminating with his poignant, closing mantra.

A Magical Conversation

The alchemy of this initial part of the scene resides in the metamorphosis of the individualities of the four characters, Maria, Philia,

Astrid and Luna into what Steiner refers to as an 'egoity'. Steiner is rightly adamant to insist that the three friends of Maria are individual characters in their own right, and not representatives of the sentient soul, the intellectual soul and the consciousness soul. This is important, and it may be difficult initially to concur with Steiner here. In the first scene when each of the other characters gives us something of their background, we learn little of these three individuals, so when we encounter them in this scene it is easy to think of them as representatives. The fact that they demonstrate here to us these soul aspects does not, however, define them. In real life, a teacher may talk like a teacher (many do) and a policeman like a policeman etc. This does not fully delineate them as people—such is the case with Philia, Astrid and Luna. This configuration is, of course, unique in drama and demands a certain flexibility of thinking on our part. The 'egoity' is as if all are part of one individuality.

When one thinks of a more ordinary group of individuals, they, in a sense, lose some of their personal uniqueness when working together as a collective and certain traits may particularly come to the fore. In the case of these four characters, they correspond to The Beautiful Lily and her three handmaidens in Goethe's story. Their beauty symbolizes a very high level of spiritual development. One can sense Goethe's enjoyment in the writing of those passages concerning Lily and her attendants: similarly in the play, the beauty of the language creates a warm, exhilarating mood in the audience. Steiner tells us that the rhythm of the language[2] tells much about the soul forces. In translation—no matter how accurate or artistic—something of this is inevitably lost, however, we can live into the moods of the speeches and allow them to work into our feelings and creative faculties as well as our cognition.

Maria initially addresses each member of the egoity individually. (The reader will find their characteristics further described in the section regarding the characters.) Philia is addressed as, 'my Philia', Astrid is, 'beloved mirror image of my spirit', demonstrating their inherent connectivity here with Maria. This is similarly the case with Luna. As the will force of the consciousness soul, she is invited to:

> join with your sisters' gifts
> the image of your own uniqueness.[3]

So a convivial dialogue emerges with Maria interacting with what, in this scene itself, have in essence—although remembering Steiner's aforesaid warning—become her soul forces. Whilst enjoying the artistic achievement of this dialogue, one can learn much from reading and re-reading it:

> The speeches at the beginning of Scene Seven are a better description of sentient soul, intellectual soul and consciousness soul than any number of words otherwise would achieve.[4]

To attempt paraphrasing or 'analysis' of the content would be prosaic and pedantic—the characters speak to each of us in an individual way.

The Ethers
Philia's element is in the sound or chemical ether:

> I will entreat the spirits of the worlds
> that they, with light of being,
> enchant soul feeling,
> that they, with tone of words,
> charm spirit hearing....[5]

Astrid's realm is that of the light and she expresses the Goethean understanding that colour is the result of the interaction of the light and the darkness:

> And I will weave
> into the radiant light
> the clouding darkness.[6]

Light has to be mitigated by the beauty of colour. Colour and form aid cognition. Luna operates in the life ether:

> I will enwarm soul substance
> And will make firm life-ether.[7]

Alchemy
Steiner's remarks about the 'alchemy' of this scene are borne out in the conversation of this 'egoity'. It has all the fascination of a kind of

ritual of a white magic sisterhood. Maria makes her requests; these are followed by the responses in turn of Philia, Astrid and Luna; this procedure is then repeated in the same order, following Maria's second speech. We are shown how the three 'soul forces' work together in harmony, each working within their limits to arouse in Johannes's soul strength for 'soaring flight'.[8] When we reflect on it, we can see just how insightful this sisterly interchange is.

Philia, the bearer of the sentient soul and the feeling element, breathes in the light. Astrid, who embodies the intellectual or mind soul, and the thinking element, condenses the light. Astrid weaves in the light ether, but pure light dazzles and she has to create the power of darkness to allow the colours to materialize. Then, finally, they are made firm by Luna with her will-forces of the consciousness soul. Philia works in the sound ether. We are shown how Philia takes in the sound, Astrid harmonizes it and Luna implants it.

Nature spirits

The second part of the conversation references the nature spirits or elementals. The element of Philia is water, where we find the undines,

> elemental spirits of the watery element... They live in the etheric element of water, swimming and floating in it.[9]

Astrid's element is the air, frequented by the sylphs:

> Because air is everywhere imbued with light, these sylphs living in the element of air and warmth press towards the light and become related to it.[10]

Warmth is the element of Luna and she is associated with the fire spirits or salamanders , who inhabit the element of heat and light.

> Just as the sylphs gather up the light, so do the fire spirits gather up the warmth and carry it unto the flowers of the plant.[11]

Enter Johannes

Just as the poetry of despair in scene two needed to be toned down through the entrance of the reassuring Maria, so the lyricism of this rhapsodical conversation has to slightly deflate—we cannot stay in lyrical mode too long. The prosaic greeting, 'Maria it is you', brings us a step away from our erstwhile reverie. Johannes is joyful, and affords a recapitulation of events. This is truly an epiphany for him—a moment when former doubts are put to flight as he recognizes Maria in the spirit world. Previously he was uncertain as to the true nature of his spiritual experiences.

This freedom from the fetters of the sense world with its limitations he has gained through his suffering. He continues:

> … My suffering then
> has brought abundant fruit.
> It has now freed me from the phantom being
> that I had formed from out myself
> and that has held me prisoner.
> I could attain to you on paths of soul
> and this I owe to pain.[12]

Maria asks him to recount his experiences and his lengthy résumé allows the audience an opportunity to take stock of the situation prior to the dramatic revelation of Theodora. He notes that those who are filled with spirit, Felix and Felicia, appeared as themselves, unlike Strader and Capesius whose ages differed from earthly reality. His advancement affords a sense of completion at this point in the play, however, Johannes still has a long way to travel in his spiritual development. He is yet to pass the Guardian of the Threshold. He has, however, emerged triumphant from all his suffering.

Johannes describes his meeting with Maria in terms which show a spiritual aspect to his love for her:

> Not earthly was your being,—
> I clearly recognized
> the spirit in your soul.
> It did not act as does a human being
> within a sentient body;
> it acted as a spirit
> who gives existence to those deeds
> that have their roots within eternity.[13]

The beautiful Lily is no longer unreachable and their relationship is strengthened. This is enhanced by the revelation of Theodora.

Enter Theodora

Her entry is as dramatic as it was in scene one and again her opening words, 'I am impelled to speak', alert us to the fact that cosmic forces are instigating the revelations. Maria, the soul forces and Theodora all have golden haloes, but Theodora, the hawk in the tale, alone has wings. The audience knows, having experienced her previous revelation and its effect on Strader, that another new door is opening. Her vision of the Hibernian incarnation in which Maria is the Christ messenger, Johannes the woman who falls at his feet, and Maria's child the hostile pagan, illustrates the mechanisms whereby the karmic forces created in past incarnations vigorously impel our actions in subsequent life.

Johannes is unable to prevent himself from falling to his knees before Maria. The karmic knot referred to by Benedictus becomes apparent. The hostility of the child in the previous incarnation is the root cause of Maria's difficult relationship with him. The devotion of the woman to the Christ messenger is the underlying force which has impelled Johannes's ignoring of his former lover to join with Maria. The on-stage relationship between Maria and Johannes gave Steiner the possibility to reference these intimate areas of human relationships.

Maria

Johannes, and the audience, at this point still need an explanation from Maria as to exactly what happened to her in scene three. The audience last saw her apparently cursing Benedictus. Maria's lengthy speech makes further demands on the actress, for whom this is a challenging scene. Her narrative conjures further her empathy with Johannes, and ushers the feeling of spiritual richness, enhancing the soul-mood for the entrance of Benedictus.

She explains Johannes's suffering for his and the audience's benefit:

> Your pain increased to overflowing
> through presence of so many people.
> With them you are united through strength of destiny,

and so the revelation of their beings
could shake your heart so deeply.
Karma has gathered them about you now
to wake in you a power
that helped your life progress.[14]

The length of the first scene is thus explained—such a number of people, with whom he is karmically related, was required to initially cause Johannes to suffer as he did. The suffering awoke in him the necessary power. Maria's relationship with Johannes has always been strong. It is now developing further:

Since you stand closest to my soul
and have kept faith to me through all your pain,
it therefore is my lot
to bring to its completion
the consecration blessing you with light.[15]

She then relates how when Benedictus told her of her special mission, her soul was filled with 'blissfulness' and her true being took flight into the spirit world where Johannes has now found her.

Benedictus
Benedictus now appears. As orchestrator of this magical scene he has something reminiscent of Prospero in Shakespeare's, *The Tempest*, however, it is Maria and Johannes who make their own decisions in these processes. Steiner always insisted on complete freedom for the pupils of spiritual science. True to his name, Benedictus gives his benediction upon their relationship:

You have been joined by destiny
together to unfold the powers
which are to serve the good in active work...
The spirit's guidance has united you in knowledge;
so now unite yourselves for spirit work.[16]

He leaves us with a lovely mantra, which can be compared with the one at the end of scene three. They are to be found in Appendix 2 in both English and German.

This scene is one of the most memorable and beautiful in all the Mystery Dramas. As Rudolf Steiner said:

> Because they show themselves so clearly in the Devachan scene, everything in it is alchemy in the purest sense of the word; all of alchemy is there if one can gradually discover it.[17]

The Interlude

*'It is where the powers of creation
have left the world of matter
unfinished that man can apply
his creative striving.'*

Sophia[1]

After the triumphant revelries of the Devachan scene, we have to come down to earth once more. There usually follows an interval at this point in the proceedings. The Interlude is set in the prosaic surrounds of Sophia's room and the language is in prose. Domesticity is underlined with Sophia's reference to being, 'busy with the children'. Artistically, it is essential for the dramatist to settle us in such earthly realms.

The Composition of the Play
The play is deliberately calibrated. As we have seen, from the prose of the Prelude we moved into the poetic setting of the scenes of the play. From the discussion in Scene One, which mirrored the argument of the Prelude, we moved through the gears with the heightened language of Scene Two, the ethereal wonders of the astral world and finally the lyricism of Scene Seven. The second half of the play repeats this process, moving from the prose of the Interlude to the triumph of the Sun Temple. The visual aspect of the play becomes similarly heightened as we progress from Sophia's room to the Sun Temple. The Prologue and the Interlude are integral to this process.

Estella's Visit
Whilst Sophia's group have been enacting the first seven scenes, Estella has seen a drama which followed a similar plot – the artist, 'haunted' by guilt at having jilted his lover, who died of grief, and suffering unrequited love from a woman who has helped him develop his talents, 'ended in utter despair'. This ending is where the Mystery Drama begins. Estella is a vivacious melancholic who, as a girl, Sophia informs us, 'suffered intensely' at other's misfortunes.

We can enter into her feelings of empathy – again, Pusch's sharp observation that there is both a Sophia and an Estella within each of us is brought to mind.

The conversation is finely balanced. Estella's energy and enthusiasm for *The Uprooted* ensure that she initially takes charge. She desperately wants to share her feelings with her friend. She makes no enquiries about Sophia's endeavours. She is very much taken up by her own pre-occupations, waxing lyrical about the dramatic construction of the play. Sophia listens with sympathy and tact:

> I have always admired writers who could
> represent what you call the faithfulness to life;
> and it seems to me that particularly nowadays
> many have achieved a mastery in this.[2]

She is referring here to Zola, Ibsen, Strindberg, Chekhov and others of that particular era; screenwriters and novelists of today have similar aims and work within a similar framework of 'realism' – imitating daily life. Sophia moves gradually to the interesting and, initially possibly puzzling, feeling of 'uneasiness' she has about much realistic art, and 'other schools too'.

> This happens when I become aware
> of what I would call the untruthfulness,
> in a deeper sense, of various works of art.[3]

At this point, Sophia has taken control of the conversation. The untruthfulness she refers to is revealed in the description of *The Uprooted* – it consists of the omission of those aspects that we have seen in *The Portal of Initiation* – karma, the spirit world, etc. Reduction rather than deception is the problem. The mere imitation of nature is 'senseless':

> When even the most imperfect rendering
> of what lies hidden from external
> observation may prove to be a revelation.[4]

Estella is unable to concur with this line of reasoning – her wish to share her enjoyment of the play she has seen has been thwarted. Sophia's final pronouncement on the subject is not something Estella is able to refute rationally:

> That is just why so many works of
> art are unsatisfying. A creative person
> is led by the creative activity itself beyond Nature –
> but he does not yet know the appearance
> of anything that lies beyond his sense
> perception.[5]

Estella disappointedly retires from the fray hoping their friendship 'will see better times'. They depart still friends. The audience is left in thoughtful, mild amusement.

Scene Eight

'To learn to know our being
we first must find that power in ourselves
that as true spirit
is able to conceal itself from us.'

Capesius.[1]

The descent into the prose of the Interlude marks a change of direction as we move into the poetics of the latter half of the play. The final scene takes place, as in the tale, in the temple 'at the surface of the earth', having moved from its 'subterranean' location in scene five. Retardus (the Mixed King) is defeated. The focus, however, in the four final scenes, is much more upon the development of the individual characters.

There is a change in the atmosphere of the play at this juncture. 'The knot that karma spins',[2] becomes the operational motif for these concluding scenes and the following three dramas. The settings of the next three scenes are those of the first three scenes. The heightened poetry of scenes four to seven is not replicated—we are much more in the realm of individual development and the drama of the individual psyche.

The action of scene eight transpires three years after the preceding scenes. The development of Johannes has proceeded apace, as Professor Capesius relates at the beginning of the scene. Johannes became the professor's pupil, taking much interest in his lectures. Previously Johannes was more inward looking; this scene demonstrates his interest in the development of others, especially Capesius with whom he has struck up a friendship.

Johannes's artistic abilities have also noticeably developed. As Capesius observes:

Each of your pictures was for me a fresh surprise.[3]

This progress of their colleague has quietly but clearly impacted on both Capesius and Strader—who are no longer Wisps. Strader remarks:

Thomasius is for me a marvel.[4]

They refer to Johannes as Thomasius, rather than Johannes, in this scene, possibly referencing the change they perceive in him. They revert back to 'Johannes' later. In the tale, the Wisps become helpers rather than disrupters—albeit without losing their playfulness. Capesius and Strader simply lose their wispiness; this scene particularly indicates their development from an individual perspective. They each require experiences, but different kinds of soul experiences, to rid them of their doubts.

The development of Johannes is a fact, and as we have previously observed, facts impress Strader. The discussion about Johannes's picture commences with a comment from Capesius which directly refers us back to Sophia's observation that an artist often, 'does not yet know the appearance of anything that lies beyond his sense perception'.[5] Capesius relates that he had previously felt it presumptuous to approach spiritual realms, but to Johannes he confides:

> I've heard you say repeatedly,
> you owe your powers in art
> entirely to that gift
> of consciously perceiving other worlds,—
> that you can put
> into your paintings nothing
> but what you've first beheld in spirit.[6]

His next sentence shows how far Capesius himself has moved away from his previous expressions of Wispy scepticism:

> I see how in your work the spirit
> can actively reveal itself.[7]

This declaration by the Platonist, Capesius, whose inward reflections on Johannes and his work, coupled with Felicia's nourishing tales, have brought about this realization, disturbs Doctor Strader:

> I've never understood you less.
> In every artist, spirit surely
> has livingly expressed itself.
> What then distinguishes
> Thomasius from other masters?[8]

Capesius replies that Johannes paints, 'what he can consciously perceive in spirit'. Strader continues to admire the picture and admits that although he has been well acquainted with Capesius for some years:

> The portrait shows me clearly
> how little I have really known of him.[9]

Johannes later reveals to Maria that his vision of Capesius in the soul world, as a young man revealed:

> capacities of this life that declared
> themselves the sequel of a former life on earth.[10]

He goes on to reveal:

> My brush was guided
> by forces which Capesius unfolded
> from former lives on earth.[11]

Although Johannes has not yet seen into a previous incarnation of Capesius, he is able to depict soul forces that would not generally be apparent to most portrait painters. Interestingly Johannes concludes by saying:

> As work of art I do not rate it highly.[12]

He is perhaps warning that spiritual experiences do not necessarily produce great art, or feeling that he needs greater insights.

Strader, however, has been shocked. The staging of such a shock process—which in life might take some weeks or more to register—is challenging for the actor. This is a dramatic turning point for Strader; however, melodrama must not creep in. The crux of the problem with which Strader has to grapple is his need to deny Johannes's spirit vision—or certainly his ability to access it and consciously render it artistically. Strader is confronted by this portrait in front of his own eyes. Many people have commented on the way the portraits of Rembrandt live in the light and when viewed together in a gallery room, are like living presences.

Such works of art have a magical feel to them, as seems to be the case here. This causes distress to Strader:

> O all these colours—they are only surface,
> and yet they're not.
> It is as if they're only visible
> to make themselves invisible to me.[13]

The man who rejected what he saw as the rituals and superstitions of the cloister for the certainties of science cannot bear magic. He must fight to keep his reason:

> I cannot understand
> whereto this picture's driving me.[14]

An arresting metaphor of the impotence of materialism against such apparently inexplicable forces arises when he despairs:

> The canvas,—I would like to break it through
> to find what I should look for.[15]

The way that the colours and forms, 'speak of the spirit's weaving', is not, for Strader, the pleasing paradox of most gallery visitors; it becomes an attack—a full, frontal attack on his whole conceptual framework:

> A spirit power creates within the artist
> as it creates within the tree or stone.[16]

The idea that the artist can 'penetrate it with cognition',[17] or work consciously within this spirit realm is a nightmarish refutation of Strader's whole standpoint.

Capesius shrewdly tells Strader to:

> Believe but good
> of such a moment.[18]

His own experiences have shown him that such a challenge to the primacy of the rational are health-giving and, although disturbing, beneficial. Although Strader seemed to have 'lost' himself in a certain sense, in actual fact,

> you were raised above yourself.[19]

The professor understands the nature of the trial his friend is experiencing. The erstwhile Wisps exit and Maria comments:

> Capesius is closer far to spirit knowledge
> than he himself is yet aware,
> and Strader suffers deeply.
> His spirit cannot find
> what ardently his soul is looking for.[20]

Whilst this seems an accurate assessment at this juncture, one may feel that although the depths in Strader are less easily penetrable than is the soul of Capesius, Strader has arrived at an awareness of reincarnation by his own efforts. Some movement too has occurred in his soul forces as a result of the shocks of the seeress's vision and the picture.

Capesius has certainly come on a journey:

> Now I perceive that ancient word of wisdom
> 'Know thou thyself' in a new light.
> To learn to know our being,
> we first must find that power in ourselves,
> that as true spirit
> is able to conceal itself from us.[21]

Maria's reply prepares us for scene nine:

> To find ourselves, we must unfold that power first
> that penetrates into our inmost being.
> The word of wisdom says in truth:
> Evolve yourself, in order to behold yourself.[22]

The scene demonstrates how the characters have grown more closely together during the three years since the previous scene. Johannes and Maria express keen interest in their colleagues, Strader and Capesius (no longer Wisps). Johannes and Capesius have forged a strong friendship. Strader is, to an extent, forging his own path, having realized the possibility of reincarnation and karma, but, too expresses his admiration of Johannes and closeness to Capesius, who has an almost avuncular affection for him. The relationships, whose karmic nature is explored throughout the dramas, are of central importance to each individual.

Scene Nine

'O man unfold your being...
I want to feel these words' full power,
although they sound so gently.
They shall become for me a quickening fire
in my soul forces
and on my spirit paths.'

Johannes.[1]

The previous scene has shown the admiration of Capesius, Strader and, indeed, Maria for the development of Johannes. Maria refers to his spiritual connectivity as, 'the wellspring of such greatness'. In scene nine Johannes himself articulates his vision, composure and hopes. It is a compositional counterpoint to the second scene in which the turmoil of his Kamaloka experience of the girl he deserted and his revelation of his lower self were expressed.

Scene two interrupts the correspondence of the play with the fairy-tale narrative. For the purposes of the play, Johannes's character needs to be explored; the Prince in the tale is a rather more passive character, swept along by the action of the story. The following scenes prior to the Interlude restore that narrative, however, the second half of the play delves further into the progress of the individuals, especially its main character, Johannes.

Scenes two and nine expand upon the tradition of the soliloquy in drama. The dialogues are conducted by Johannes with his own interior landscape and continue for almost the duration of the scene, concluding only with the calming presence of Maria. The Chorus of the rocks and springs signifies changes of nuance, changes of direction or of emphasis. It brings a musical, reverberative quality which echoes on in the souls of the audience.

The difference between a Mystery Drama and an ordinary play is emphatically brought to our attention in these scenes. In scene two, the experience normally undergone after crossing the threshold of death, opens spiritual vistas for Johannes and for the audience. He gazes inward; the process of development, which we now witness three years later, allows his vision to flow outward. We too, share some of the spiritual elation he feels, but the rhythmic sequence and the intervention of Maria allow us a necessary distancing, a space for thoughtful reflection and evaluation.

The landscape setting, which we think of as taking place in the soul of Johannes and the outpourings which flow from him throw searchlight beams into his psyche, laying it bare before our eyes. The demands on the actor are immense. We must be kept engaged, but not overpowered by his emotions.

The need to look inward in scene two—know thyself—and to examine one's thoughts and deeds objectively and consciously, a gesture of self-awareness, becomes in scene nine an outward unfolding of 'I and the world'. Doubt and self-loathing have become self-confidence and self-realization; the recognition of guilt is replaced by the need to redeem it.

The Word

The German phrase, *'O Mensch, erlebe dich'* is literally translated by Adam Bittleston as, 'O Man, experience yourself'. This seems both concise and comprehensive. Collison uses, 'O man, feel thou thyself.' Pusch chose, 'O man, unfold your being', reasoning that it is active and carrying, 'a gesture which implies an over-emphasis of self, the luciferic aberration to which Johannes is drawn in the following scene'. As Pusch goes on to state, 'The words themselves preserve, too, the significant sound-sequence L-B of the original.'[2]

Johannes expresses an imaginative vision of the heights to which he will reach. He is entitled, after all the battles he has fought, to feel a sense of being on the right track, however, he has not yet passed the Guardian of the Threshold and, as Pusch indicates, is prone to illusion, not having reached further than imaginative cognition.[3] He utters no cautions, or assertions of the difficulties which lie ahead; his vulnerability to deception is therefore tested by Lucifer in the following scene.

The Counterpoint

To have two scenes with such direct interaction as these two Rock Spring scenes contributes well to the compositional unity of the drama. As the spiritual development of Johannes became the prime focus, scene two breaking the fairy-tale narrative was required; its counterpoint in scene nine harmonizes the composition. The complexity of each of these two scenes forms a mirror image; we still have questions in our minds about Johannes at the end of them. Comparing the language of scene two and scene nine is a satisfying process. The first lines of them show an immediate contrast:

> Scene Two   *O man, know thou thyself.*
>   For many years these words
>   of weighty meaning I have heard.
>   They sound to me from air and water;
>   they echo up from depths of earth.[4]

Johannes is the receiver; he is acted upon by the deep, heavy resonance of 'these words'. The years are 'many'; the meaning 'weighty'. Conversely in scene nine, Johannes is the active seeker:

> O man, unfold your being!
> For three years now I've sought
> for power of soul, with wings of
> courage,
> to give these words their truth.[5]

The thrust is outward; the 'power' and 'wings of courage' signal a positive seeking of strength. The speaker in the second scene is desperately searching:

> And just as in the acorn secretly
> the structure of the mighty oak is pressed.[6]

'Secretly' implies that which is deliberately hidden away, hard to access. 'Pressed' indicates confinement or constriction. The corresponding lines in scene nine:

> Just as the tiny acorn
> mysteriously can expand
> into the giant body of the noble oak.[7]

create a sense of wonder. Mysteries can delight, secrets can frustrate. The 'giant body of the noble oak' personifies the tree in an endearing, but revering manner; 'expand' enhances the idea of unfolding, reaching outward.

In scene two, 'darkness'[8] weaves around Johannes and 'as raging dragon I must see myself'.[9] The imagery is that of horror and terror. In scene nine, 'There lives in me the light'.[10] The being that he saw in scene two was 'from the dark abyss';[11] in scene nine: 'From light-filled heights a Being shines on me.'[12] The uncertainty that Johannes expressed in scene two:

> But every moment can
> deprive me of myself.[13]

is replaced by certainty in his final scene nine speech:

> Maria, are you then aware
> of what has just revealed itself?
> For me man's core of confidence,
> for me the certainty of being has been won.
> I feel indeed the power of the words
> which everywhere can guide me:
> O man unfold your being![14]

Maria's awareness stems from the fact that:

> So closely are we linked
> that your soul's life
> lets its light shine into my soul.[15]

Gradually 'the knot that karma spins' has more light shed upon it. Maria's presence helps and inspires Johannes:

> My soul has led me here.
> I could behold your star:
> it shines in its full power.[16]

In the following play Johannes will need to become more independent—but not yet!

Scene Ten

'Light of whose fullness
men, when seeing,
in truth are thinking;
light from whose fullness
men, when striving,
in love are living.'

           Voice of Spirit from the Heights. [1]

One has a strong feeling that the writing of this scene, with all its twists and turns must have given pleasure to the dramatist. All writers enjoy playing tricks and providing surprises. There is, however, a deeply serious purpose to the deceptions which entertain the audience; they reveal Johannes's vulnerability to illusions—and ours!

This scene, like the previous one, continues to explore the spiritual progress of the main character and is free of references to Goethe's tale. (One may, perhaps, detect a certain Faustian element.) The dramatic occurrences change the previous mood, setting the audience on its toes after our sharing Johannes's joy in his achievements. It is a necessary scene—without it we would be under the impression that Johannes had finally triumphed and in fairy-tale style, lived happily ever after. Life being more challenging, however, we *have* to see the cunning of the forces of adversity and the fact that just when we feel triumphant we are at our most vulnerable. Steiner reiterates the warnings of Estella in the Prelude against smugness and complacency.

Theodosius appears in spirit garb and we, the audience, assume, as does Johannes, that he is the benevolent hierophant, brother of Benedictus. We need to remind ourselves how Lucifer worked through the beautiful Helena in scene one. The previous vision of the brotherhood in the temple (scene five) aids Lucifer in his deception. Johannes ironically affirms:

> You stood before my spirit-gaze within the temple,
> though then I could not yet be sure
> if dream or truth appeared to me.
> But lifted is the veil

> that kept the light of spirit hid from me.
> I know now you are real.[2]

Johannes is being approached after his victories in the previous scene—at such times of rejoicing, we are prone to slacken our guard. The words, 'joy' and 'happiness' are uttered by Theodosius in his opening speech and repeated in Johannes's reply. The audience shares Johannes's confusion; we too have seen Theodosius as the good hierophant—the 'brother' of Benedictus in the Maya Temple of scene five. Johannes, again with unconscious irony, refers to his gratitude to Benedictus. Theodosius then urges Johannes to feel him in 'depths of soul'[3] and gushes:

> In deeds of love you shall partake of blessedness.[3]

Lucifer's strength and power is manifest as Johannes says:

> I feel your presence gives me warming light.
> I feel creative power arising in me.[4]

On the disappearance of Theodosius, Johannes initially feels 'uplifted', then it seems to him as if an evil spirit is approaching. He soliloquizes that he has, 'the strength to set myself against it'. He feels sure; he tells the audience, that 'the fiercest adversary—will find me armed'. [5] Benedictus then appears! A dramatic moment! Johannes initially believes him to be an imposter:

> O come to life, good forces of my soul
> and shatter the illusion
> desiring to ensnare me.[6]

Momentarily the audience too is unsure. The calm voice of Benedictus who simply points out to Johannes, 'what through these years my presence meant to you', still leaves Johannes, and ourselves, in some doubt:

> O he has left me.
> And whether I've dispelled illusion …

> or a reality has left me …
> how can I tell?[7]

The real difficulties of luciferic delusion are brought home to the audience. Benedictus is also able to spiritually energize Johannes, and at this point Johannes decides correctly and momentarily realizes the truth:

> And yet I feel myself grown stronger.
> It was not an illusion but he himself.[8]

He comes to terms with his own gullibility:

> And yet … I just succumbed to strong illusion.
> I felt with horror your approach
> and could regard you as deception
> although you stood before me.[9]

The Lord of Desire, however, persists; we watch nonplussed as Theodosius reappears. He astutely tempts Johannes to augment the work of Benedictus, appealing to the artist's ego:

> If you experience only
> what he has placed in you,
> you cannot then unfold yourself.[10]

The last line refers us back to the triumphs and resolutions of the last scene. Theodosius finishes with a flourish:

> In freedom strive into the light-filled heights.
> Receive my strength now for this striving.[11]

Johannes again is elated. The boundless joy he feels at Theodosius's promises and the vistas of light they allow him to anticipate are again underpinned by the previous vision of the 'Maya Temple ' of scene five:

> So work on further in my soul's foundations
> sublime, majestic words.

> You must have had your origin in the temple,
> since Benedictus's brother uttered you.[12]

Lucifer's seductions are like a magnet to the ego of Johannes, drawing him into dreamy delusion. He is so sure; he will draw out of himself the creative spirit of his higher self. We then have another dramatic moment—the appearance is that of Lucifer and Ahriman.

It is interesting, and informative, to compare their speeches to those in scene four. The two introductory lines have changed:

Scene 4	Scene 9
Lucifer: 'O man, know yourself.'	'O man, know me'
'O man, experience me.	'O man, sense yourself.'
Ahriman: 'O man, know me.'	'O man, know yourself.'
'O man, experience yourself.'	'O man sense me.'

The following half-a-dozen lines are the same but the quatrain preceding the final two lines, in each instance contains a virulent threat rather than the positive language of the previous encounter. Johannes has advanced and requires more than sweet talk:

Lucifer gloats:

> You will find alien being
> in the wide regions of the heights.
> It will confine you
> to human fate.
> It will oppress you.[13]

Ahriman menaces:

> I harden solid ground.
> You can, however, lose it.
> By vacillating you disperse
> the power of being.
> And you can squander
> in lofty light
> the strength of spirits.
> You can disintegrate.[14]

Johannes not only sees Ahriman and Lucifer, but can recognize that they have emanated from his own self. It was a necessary lesson to both Johannes and to ourselves. The drama of the scene has kept us enthralled and we may smile with relief. The 'Voice of the Spirit from the Heights' takes us into the realm of the light—the light of wisdom which has been a persistent theme since the children's singing in the Prelude. Johannes is now ready to move into the Sun Temple. The Voice of the Spirit from the Heights may be compared with the 'Spirit Voice' at the end of scene three. The message in the latter refers to the third person, 'him'; this becomes 'you':

Scene 3   Scene 9

'World of whose fullness...'	becomes	'Light of whose fullness...'
'men, when thinking',	becomes	'men when seeing',
'dream in shadows';		'in truth are thinking';
'world from whose fullness...'		'light from whose fullness...'
'men, when seeing',		'men, when striving',
'live with phantoms'.		'in love are living'.

Scene Eleven—The Final Scene

'The sacrifice you bring the temple
shall here be re-enacted in my soul.
In me the warmth of love shall sacrifice
itself unto the light of love.'
Johannes (to The Other Maria).[1]

The final scene of a Shakespeare comedy will see all the loose ends tidied. Couples will be happily united ever after and we can leave the theatre with warm hearts and smiling faces. The final scene of *The Portal of Initiation*, cannot quite give us this feeling. It has to complete the fairy tale—which would, of its own accord, allow us such unmitigated pleasure—Retardus is defeated and the Temple has risen to the surface. The other strand, and the primary pre-occupation of the play, the individual development of the characters, leaves a more ambiguous feeling.

Spiritual Realism does not easily enter the happily-ever-after bed-chamber. There are, inevitably, still questions to be addressed. Many lessons have been learned and a vast anthroposophical syllabus has been covered. The play itself is a lifetime study. As in life itself, questions remain unanswered regarding the spiritual development of the characters.

Is Johannes free of illusions? Will Strader cast aside his doubt? Capesius seems in a better place—as do all the characters—than when the play commenced, but what is next for him? All these questions— and more besides—set us up nicely for the following dramas.

The climax of the play deftly unites the finale of the fairy tale with the focus on the individual development of the characters, which has clearly become the primary objective of the dramatist. We are reminded of Steiner's words:

> Each person is a 'Johannes Thomasius' in his own fashion. Everything in the drama is presented, therefore, in a completely individual way. Through this, the truth portrayed by the particular figures brings out as clearly as possible the development of the soul of a human being.[2]

The fairy story provides an ending in which the bridge, facilitated by the sacrifice made by the Green Snake, unites the earthly and the spiritual world. There cannot be a correspondingly communal solution in the drama. We all have to find our own bridge, or spiritual path.

Other aspects of the conclusion of the tale are rendered in the devachanic vision of the final scene of the play. Interestingly, whilst Hutchins attributes the scene in the Sun Temple as being, 'Johannes's prophetic vision of the future', [3] Collison with equal clarity tells us that it, 'must be thought of as taking place in the soul of Maria'. [4] Maria is clearly much further advanced along the spiritual path than Johannes, so it seems likely that Collison, who had access to Steiner, is correct, although the other scenes have been the meditations of Johannes.

The defeat of Retardus corresponds to the fate of the Mixed King in the tale, who is also a reactionary. The relationship of Johannes and Maria, which has become closer and obstacle-free, mirrors that of the Prince and the Lily. The temple itself is no longer 'subterranean'. In the story it dramatically journeys to the earth's surface—the final scene of the play, unable to facilitate such 'special effects', is situated in the realm of spiritual vision. The Other Maria, the Green Snake, does not appear in the following plays—hers has been the major sacrifice, and her soul qualities are now in unity with those of her namesake.

The temple of the Sun, as Collison indicates, may be likened to the perfect human heart, the 'sun' organ. The hierophants are resplendent in their robes: 'Benedictus wears a long, white robe over which is a broad, golden stole with mystic emblems in red. He also wears a golden mitre and carries a golden crosier … Theodosius is similarly robed except that the stole, mitre and crosier are silver and the emblems are blue … The stole, mitre and crosier of Romanus are bronze and the emblems are green. Retardus's costume is a mixture of the other three.' [5]

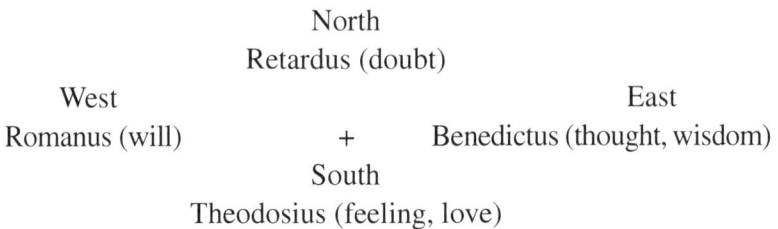

North
Retardus (doubt)

West   East

Romanus (will)   +   Benedictus (thought, wisdom)

South
Theodosius (feeling, love)

The Triumph of the Wisps

The fate of Retardus is sealed (he does not appear in the following dramas), through the failure of Capesius and Strader to lead Johannes and Maria into doubt and scepticism. He endowed Capesius with powers of erudition to convince, and Strader with mental clarity with which to sow doubt. They failed so to do.

Their refusal is the culmination of the discourse regarding material science and spiritual science begun in the Prelude, continued in the first scene with the Wisps arguing against Maria's 'egoity', and on into the thunder and lightning of the astral world and finally the discussion of the portrait of Capesius. From their testiness in scene one, their attitudes have mellowed—Capesius affirming his belief in the spiritual world, and Strader now doubting his own scepticism. Capesius tells Retardus that he has been able to interest people and teach them, but found himself unable to fire their spirits.

Strader then succinctly refutes Retardus, using his kindly donated mental clarity to expose the dullness and lack of inspiration of the hierophant:

> The weakness into which I had to fall
> is but the image of your own.
> You could confer upon me knowledge,
> but not the power to silence all the longing
> which strives within man's heart for truth.[6]

We may be reminded of Philia's words in reply to Strader in scene one:

> Such words will always come
> from knowledge that has been achieved
> through dry, prosaic reason.[7]

Ahriman and Lucifer

The following discussion between Benedictus and Ahriman and Lucifer helps in our understanding of the roles played by each of the adversarial powers. This drama—the first portrayal of them on stage—gives an extra dimension to our comprehension of them, and paves the way for further exploration in the following plays.

They show themselves here as, 'the necessary powers of hindrance'. When Benedictus makes clear to Lucifer that Johannes and Maria are aware of his presence, Lucifer says he must, 'indeed release their souls'.[8] Lucifer can only work fruitfully upon those who are unaware of his presence. For those who have such an awareness, his power to hinder is relinquished and he becomes a positive force:

> But still my might remains,
> allotted to me in world becoming.
> And although I may not tempt their souls,
> yet in the spirit shall my power
> let ripen for them fruits of greatest beauty.[9]

Those final three lines are a reminder that Lucifer is also the inspirer of not only art and philosophy, but all such vehicles which lift our souls away from the material world. Similarly Benedictus indicates to Ahriman that Maria and Johannes have overcome that shadowy, materialistic way of thinking that precludes the spiritual origins of life on earth:

> Johannes and Maria's souls
> have conquered error's darkness in themselves.
> Their eyes of spirit they have opened.[10]

Ahriman reluctantly renounces 'their spirit', but again we are shown that he, too, is an inspirer and not simply an adversary:

> And yet it will not be denied me
> still further to delight their souls
> with shine of semblance.
> They will not any longer
> believe it to be truth,
> but they will have the power to see
> how semblance manifests the truth.[11]

The final two lines show the value and rightful task of Ahriman. Ahriman's duties include the overseeing of the lifeless mineral world, and the rightful regulation of the necessity of death. He is the inspirer of materialistic science and its wonders. The immense difficulties for individuals to ensure that Lucifer and Ahriman are restricted to their rightful tasks are explored further in the following Mystery Dramas.

None Should Act Alone
The following dialogues involve The Other Maria, the Green Snake, whose decision, along with that of Felix, to tread the path of knowledge and love to the temple, rather than acting alone from goodness of heart, has like the sacrifice of the Snake, been of pivotal importance. The inter-dependence of the members of the group is strongly emphasized. Theodosius could only bestow, 'light of love',[12] (cognition and understanding) on Maria, but not the warmth of feeling. Maria's inability to help her friend and her child has been remedied. The Other Maria's soul forces were only working through unconscious impulses. Theodosius tells her:

> The influence of the temple does not reach
> to motives rooted in blind instincts
> however much good they wish to do.[13]

Through The Other Maria's understanding of the need to help the temple, Maria's 'soul light' can now be strengthened for the benefit of humanity:

> You grant me through your insight power
> to give Maria's soul light to the worlds.[14]

Johannes
The progress of Johannes is also facilitated by The Other Maria and Felix coming to the temple. Maria, his guide, has been enabled to help him. He tells The Other Maria;

> The sacrifice you bring to the temple
> shall here be re-enacted in my soul.
> In me the warmth of love shall sacrifice
> itself unto the light of love.[15]

Johannes, although more active than the Prince in the fairy tale, is similarly reliant on others in his development. In the preceding scene, Benedictus needed to remind him how reliant he was on help from his teacher. Maria now similarly reminds him how he has benefitted from her guidance:

> Johannes you have won in spirit realms
> knowledge now through me.[16]

She tells him that he needs to find his inmost soul as he found hers in the spirit world. Johannes has recognized his lower self and now needs to contact his higher ego. He has truly set foot on the path, but has not gone beyond a basic level of imaginative cognition.[17] The soul forces of Philia, Astrid and Luna bestow benevolent prophecies upon Johannes. Philia foresees his need for 'joy of soul' in the feeling realm; Astrid affirms his ability to illuminate through thinking the 'warmth of soul'[18] and Luna affirms that his will forces will allow him true individuality, 'when light can shine within your soul'.[19]

Felix

That singular individual, Felix Balde, of whom Felicia said in the first scene that he loved the solitude of his mountains so much that he would not soon make a re-appearance in the group, has joined the Temple. The reason is astutely observed by Steiner—the perceived foolishness of his fellow human beings!

> It was men's very folly that from the dark depths
> has shown to me the light
> and let me find my way into the temple.[20]

What other thought process could possibly tempt such a self-sufficient representative of the Spirit of Nature to work communally? His deep understanding of the elemental world evidenced in the first scene ensures he will be of great value to the Temple. Both Felix and The Other Maria have worked in admirable ways, but through instinct rather than cognition, and as individuals rather than in partnership with others. Romanus rebukes Felix:

> Men of your nature rob me of the power
> to give my light to earthly souls.[21]

It is not always easy to recognize and understand the need for mutual co-operation—creating 'in light' [22] rather than in 'dark depths'. [23] It is only through the entrance of The Other Maria and Felix into the Temple that Benedictus can perform the Holy Rite to wholly detach Maria and Johannes from the influence of Retardus—through whom Lucifer and Ahriman have been working. That such a highly developed individual as Maria has had to wait for the sacrifice made by The Other Maria seems incredible and gives considerable food for thought!

The Creative Art of Felicia
After Retardus laments that he has lost influence over Maria and Johannes, Felicia gives him a sharp rebuke:

> That men can kindle in themselves
> the fire for thought without your help,
> I've shown you clearly. [24]

Her fairy stories have refreshed and enlightened Capesius, and been of benefit to Strader. Such creative thinking, as also shown through Goethe's tale, can augment, bypass and transcend the prosaic dryness of the 'gifts' of Retardus. She roundly affirms:

> There streams from me a knowledge
> that's able to bear fruit. [25]

Like the Mixed King in the tale, who had the gold sucked out of him by the Wisps, Retardus has been sucked dry of his influence and authenticity:

> Capesius, my son
> you are now lost.
> You have withdrawn yourself from me
> before the temple's light can shine for you. [26]

This last foray into the belief that things are happening too quickly is sharply refuted by Benedictus, who pays tribute to the work of Felicia:

> He feels the light
> and he will win the power

> to fathom in his soul what until now
> Felicia has created for him.[27]

'I Cannot Banish Doubt'

The final dialogue between Strader and Theodora prefigures their marriage in the following plays. It hints at Strader's future development and Theodora's role in his spiritual advancement. Strader's lament, 'I cannot banish doubt itself', has echoed throughout the play, from Estella in the Prelude, to the Wisps in scene one, Retardus in the Maya Temple and Johannes in scene ten. The other doubts have been laid to rest and Theodora's vision, as she relates to Strader is that of a human image affirming:

> I have now conquered for myself
> the power to reach the light.[28]

Theodora, the Hawk in the tale, is here a voice of conscience. She tells Strader to trust in himself and prophecies that he will speak these words. Strader's spirit was much moved by Theodora's vision of the etheric Christ in scene one. We are convinced that he will be inspired by her words which immediately precede the final curtain.

The Characters

In the following chapter, I attempt to outline characteristic traits of the individualities in the drama and some of the more significant relationships. The attempt is that of a helpful guide, rather than a comprehensive survey. Each reader will, hopefully, be stimulated to discover much more in the play about the characters than can be written here. They are so many and varied that even the cast list has a richness! As the length of the first scene demonstrates, however, even providing an introductory background makes considerable demands on the powers of retention of the audience.

The characters of the first Mystery Drama are, in the main, retained for the following three plays; a few are lost, others undergo name changes; the principal nexus of Benedictus and his followers remains. This is probably the only characteristic shared by the Mystery Dramas and soap operas!

The characters are initially based on those of Goethe's fairy story, 'The Green Snake and the Beautiful Lily', which are, in turn, based on the different aspects of the human soul. Goethe afforded the higher aspects to female characters—the Snake who makes the essential sacrifices is female, as, of course is the enchanting Lily. The Will o' Wisps, who rock the boat and cause disturbances are both male. As the play proceeds, the characters become more individualized than those of the tale, and it is fascinating to see how Steiner ensures that this progression has credibility. The interplay of the alchemical spirituality of the fairy-tale elements and the harsh problems of modernity affords a unique aesthetic—charm with sharp elbows.

A Variety of Characters
The Mystery Drama involves, in addition to the pupils of Benedictus and their associates, who are ordinary men and women exploring the paths of spiritual development, other characters that are somewhat complex and utterly unfamiliar to contemporary audiences. These include 'hierophants' who seem to be rather ordinary blokes, the intriguing 'soul forces', The Spirit of the Elements, The Spirit of

the Earth Brain and the machinations of Lucifer and Ahriman. One
needs to familiarize oneself with them all, not only to understand
the play, but to enhance one's own development—the essence of the
Mystery Drama.

Such a gathering transports us into unfamiliar soul and spirit
worlds. Perseverance beyond the realms of even the most avant-
garde dramatists is needed. Even the plays and films of those such
as Samuel Beckett, Jean Luc Godard or Tarkovsky cannot rival the
drama for complexity! The rewards, however, more than repay the
effort!

Lucifer and Ahriman make their stage debut in *The Portal of Initiation*. This, in itself, makes the play remarkable. Rudolf Steiner
gave many lectures and wrote at length about the 'necessary powers
of hindrance'. My purpose in the following sections is simply that of
examining their roles in the play. The Bibliography lists some of the
lectures about these luminaries of the drama.

Characters, Actors and Audience

The movement of the play involves changes in the language, landscapes and the characters themselves. We begin in the delightfully
prosaic, domestic interior of Sophia's room, with her friend and the
children, moving in scene one to the conversation of the lecture audience, then into more imaginative realms—the Rock Spring Scene,
the astral realm and the Maya Temple, finally the spirit world of
Devachan. This compositional process is repeated in the scenes following the Interlude.

This is a progression which makes considerable demands on both
actors and audience. We move through so many changes of scene,
language and mood that simply one viewing of the play can never
be enough to take in everything. Each of the characters repays much
thought and contemplation. Steiner is pushing us to do this—and to
do it joyfully. The surprise of each scene is a pleasure as well as a
feast for thought.

Much research has been carried out by anthroposophists regarding the origins of different characters in the Mystery Dramas. This
research is interesting and some indications are given for those who
wish to follow through on this question. It is, however my belief
that each of the characters has a multiplicity of influences—they

originate in the fairy-tale characters, as well as persons known by Steiner. Crucially, each becomes an individual in their own right; Steiner absolutely insisted on this.

The Characters in the Play and the Drama

The treatment of the characters distinguishes the play from Goethe's fairy tale. In the tale, the philosophical solutions to the ills of society advanced by Schiller in his incomparable, 'Letters on the Aesthetic Education of Man' are delightfully distilled through the alchemical imaginations of Goethe into a charming work of art which indicates a communal solution—the bridge between the spiritual and material worlds made possible by the Snake's sacrifice, can be used by everyone. The Mystery Drama, whilst retaining the structure of the story focuses, particularly after the Interlude, on the individual characters and their development, exploring the interplay of their relationships.

The first and final scenes allow us to see them as a totality, reminding us of Maria's words referring to the Archetype of Man:

> It shows itself diversified in many souls,
> just as pure light, the One,
> reveals itself within the rainbow's arch
> in many-coloured hues.[1]

Throughout the play we see the contrasts (Capesius and Strader, Ahriman and Lucifer), the conflicts, the harmonious interactions of Maria, Philia, Astrid and Luna, and the progress of the individuals. Pairings and groupings afford insight after insight in the spirituality of human relationships and anthroposophical endeavours.

Johannes Thomasius

Principal Character

Johannes is the principal character in *The Portal of Initiation*, and the play focuses upon his individual development. He corresponds to the Prince in the fairy tale, however, there is a very considerable deviation regarding this particular character. The Prince is more acted upon than active—a necessarily rather two-dimensional young man who serves his function as the suitor of the Lily.

The development of Johannes, contrarily, is both complex and highly individual in nature. Rudolf Steiner stressed that it is an unusual development, but all spiritual development is by its nature uniquely individual; no two persons develop in the same way. Whilst a general guide to spiritual development such as *Knowledge of the Higher Worlds, How is it Achieved?* is a prerequisite for every seeker, it is of necessity of general usage—more abstract in nature than the experience of following the personal development of a character on the stage.

Personal Relationships

All the other characters in the play are karmically connected to Johannes. The play shows us the need for the characters to interact positively and to help each other. Personal relationships can be examined in the dramas in a more intense and intimate manner than was otherwise available to Rudolf Steiner. Throughout the dramas, Johannes's relationships with women are examined in greater depth than is the case with the other characters. We know very little, or nothing, of this aspect of the lives of Capesius and Benedictus. The effect of Theodora on Strader is remarkable, in terms of her clairvoyance challenging his earthbound thinking. In the third play their relationship is depicted, showing their mutual devotion, but again Johannes becomes involved. Other characters are less depicted in the more intimate realms of human experience.

In *The Portal of Initiation*, we learn of his unthinking and thus callous, treatment of a former lover who clearly idolized him. His intense and continuous listening to the lecture of Benedictus and the following conversations have given him insight, but led him to despair:

> What these people lack
> I know quite well;
> I also know,
> they stand in life
> and I in empty nothingness.[1]

He has to deal with karmic reparation for this relationship and throughout the following plays is reminded of the burden of his unresolved karma.

In the first drama his relationship to Maria appears entirely wholesome, and the beauty and strength of their love is conveyed. This cannot be done in the usual way with kisses and embraces; words have to suffice in the Mystery Drama. In the account which Estella gives of *The Uprooted*, a realist drama which has parallels to *The Portal of Initiation*, the artist becomes despondent because the friendly feelings of his companion, 'would never change into passionate love'. The issue is not further explored in the Mystery Drama—Maria is the very cerebral Beautiful Lily. In the following play, however, Johannes's Double shows there is a lustful element to Johannes's desires for Maria as well as the truly virtuous love which they both share. This artist is prone to the wiles of Lucifer, the Lord of Desire.

Johannes is heavily reliant upon Maria, whose development is much further forward than his. At the beginning of the Mystery Drama, we find that they have been together for ten years. Initially her help has aided considerable development in his art. A point has been reached, however, when she is unable to inspire him out of his stagnation. They require the help of their teacher, Benedictus, who understands the karmic needs of their relationship, and their development.

In scene three, the series of events begins which culminates in Johannes's recognition of Maria in the spirit world of scene seven. With the help and guidance of Benedictus, Johannes bravely retains his equanimity as Maria's physical body, having been occupied by Lucifer, hurls abuse at her mentor, Benedictus. The latter, in a lengthy speech, gives Johannes reassurance as to his having remained calm and strong throughout the previous trials. He tells him:

> Your friend has found the way.
> In spirit you will find her.[2]

He then gives further blessing to the union of Johannes and Maria with the beautiful mantra, 'Life's weaving essence radiates...' (see Appendix 2).

The Astral World and the Spirit World

Scenes four and five show Johannes the astral world with its deceptions and complexities. He has come to a recognition of his lower self in scene two and has to experience its true nature. He has not experienced his higher ego. He also has to accustom himself to crossing the threshold of the material and astral worlds.

The seventh scene marks an important stage in his development; his recognition of Maria in the spirit world affords him the firm conviction that what he is able to see in spiritual vision is reality. His previous experiences had not afforded him this certainty. When one considers the scenes in the astral world with the 'Maya Temple' and the ages of Capesius and Strader reversed, it seems reasonable that Johannes requires the certainty he celebrates in the Devachan scene.

His relationship with Maria is further strengthened by the revelation of Theodora that he was the woman who fell at the feet of 'the messenger of Christ' (Maria),[3] in the Hibernian incarnation. Johannes then 'falls to his knees before Maria'.[4] He is propelled by forces outside his control—one could almost say bewitched—certainly compelled. Maria then takes control of this dramatic moment, telling him:

> Johannes, what is dawning in you
> you must awake to full consciousness.[5]

She explains to him the karmic knot that thwarted them is becoming untied and affirms:

> Since you stand closest to my soul
> and have kept faith to me through all your pain,
> it therefore is my lot
> to bring to its completion
> the consecration, blessing you with spirit light.[6]

By the end of the first half of the play, various recognitions have come to Johannes. He has recognized not only his lower self, his need to repay karmic debts, his possibility to access genuine spiritual realms, but also the deceptions of Ahriman and Lucifer. He is certainly not immune to the latter as is illustrated in the second half and in following plays, but in the fourth scene Ahriman and Lucifer disappear, having been recognized by Johannes, and Helena has previously been rumbled.

After the Interlude

The individuality of the characters is the focus of the second half of the drama. The eighth scene provides further evidence of Johannes's development. Three years have elapsed since the Devachan scene. He has become the pupil of Capesius, thus demonstrating a more outward looking attitude to society. His development as an artist, rooted in his own ability for spiritual perception is noted by his teacher and by Strader and Maria.

Capesius gives a glowing account of how Johannes has progressed from being, 'a greatly troubled man', to an artist in whose work, 'the spirit can actively reveal itself'. Johannes now shows an interest in Capesius and Strader, especially the former:

> And if I've thus unveiled for him his inmost self,
> my picture has thus rendered
> the service which I had in mind.
> As work of art I do not rate it highly.[7]

His modesty and thoughtfulness here contrast well with his earlier self-preoccupation.

Johannes Thomasius

Interestingly, Johannes Thomasius is the only character given two first names. It is only in the eighth scene that Capesius and Strader refer to him as 'Thomasius'—during the rest of the play he is 'Johannes'. There is something of a Faustian dualism about Johannes—in future plays he becomes, like Goethe himself, both artist and scientist. Johannes is the artist, Thomasius (doubting Thomas), the scientist.

'O Man'

The second and ninth scenes fully illustrate the progress Johannes has made. They are beautifully crafted pieces of innovative drama. The correspondences are clear and to work through them systematically here would be pedantry. They do well repay such an effort. Every sentence in scene two has a counterpart in scene nine. To go through the scenes, 'side by side', as it were, is very rewarding.[8]

The feeling of desolation and wallowing in his own 'nothingness' has metamorphosed into a mood of confidence and tranquillity. In the second scene he alternates between losing himself in his surroundings—the rocks and springs of his physical and etheric bodies—and finding himself in the seclusion of his own ego. The contrast with his outlook in scene nine is stark.

The Chorus, 'O man, unfold your being', draws his affirmation:

> I find myself secure on every side,
> whenever these words' power follows me.[9]

Collison translates, '*O Mensch, erlebe dich!*' as, 'O man, feel thou thyself,' and Bittleston as, 'O man, experience thyself'.[10] The Pusch version conveys the feeling of expansion, a kind of optimism taking wing. Just as Johannes stays calm throughout the trials of the second scene, he keeps control of his exultation in scene nine. He advances from recognition to self-assurance and realizes the need to redeem his guilt for his former lover. The final speech underlines his newly acquired self-belief:

> For me, man's core of confidence
> for me, the certainty of being has been won.
> I feel indeed the power of the words

which everywhere can guide me:
O man, unfold your being![11]

Denouement: his Strengths and Future Needs

The final scenes firmly indicate Johannes's future needs—much has been achieved, but he still has far to go. He is deceived by Lucifer, speaking through Theodosius in the penultimate scene of the play. This is a deception that well illustrates the difficulties posed by Lucifer and Ahriman. The audience is initially deceived—we have seen Theodosius as 'a good guy'. Johannes's relationship with Benedictus solves the problem.

Johannes encounters Lucifer and Ahriman in this scene and realizes that they come from *himself*. In jubilation, after hearing the urgings to 'freedom' of Lucifer speaking through Theodosius, Johannes expects a beautiful spirit to come from within himself. The dramatic re-appearance of Lucifer and Ahriman, who have emerged from his own being reveal the depths of illusion to which we all are vulnerable. The Voice of the Spirit from the Heights can, however, be seen to come from Johannes's own Spirit Self. This voice prepares him for the Sun Temple.

Steiner has transformed the fairy-tale Prince into a very modern, vulnerable hero of the drama. At around 30 years of age, he is in his intellectual soul phase and wears something of the vulnerability of Hamlet. He has achieved recognition and understanding of his lower ego—that part of the ego created by Lucifer. Access to and development of the higher ego still await.

The drama, through the character of Johannes, shows us how slow and difficult spiritual progress can be even when the right methods of development are put into place. It is more than 13 years since he first joined Maria's group. He is not able to independently cross the threshold into the spiritual world and is still, in spite of the victories and insights gained and the development as a human being and an artist, very prone to error and illusion.

The Help of Others

The other characters have helped him immensely. In addition to his reliance on Maria and Benedictus, the sacrifices of The Other Maria have benefitted all. Johannes acknowledges to her:

> I could not find the way
> to reach your higher sister
> as long as warmth of love remained
> aloof from light of love in me.
> The sacrifice you bring the temple
> shall here be re-enacted in my soul.
> In me the warmth of love shall sacrifice
> itself into the light of love.[12]

Johannes needed The Other Maria and Felix Balde to find their way to the temple. The comradeship of Capesius and Strader has helped his development, and his reliance upon Maria and her 'egoity' will need to be replaced through his own striving for independence. Maria's final speech prophecies:

> Johannes, you have now beheld
> yourself in spirit through myself;
> you will as spirit experience your being
> when cosmic light beholds itself in you.[13]

Acting the Part

The challenges posed to the actor are immense. The play is more than twice the normal length of a theatre production and he is present in every scene—alone throughout most of scenes two and nine. The degree of subtlety required in a play which disallows the usual presentation of emotion is unmatched in mainstream drama.

In our time, even a Shakespeare play will allow the lovers to wildly embrace. The suffering of the hero will shake up the audience. The Mystery Drama demands tight control on the part of both actor and audience. This makes a much greater demand upon an actor than evoking tears or laughter.

Origins of the Character

The origins of the character are discussed in a fascinating article in *New View*, Winter 2020-21 by Richard Ramsbotham, who suggests Edouard Schuré as the prototype of the main character in the play. Schuré was instrumental in publicizing the more esoteric, holistic ideals of cosmic Christianity in his engagingly written book, *The Great Initiates*, and was the author of plays presented by Steiner.

Johannes can also be seen as a kind of Everyman. He has the two names 'Johannes Thomasius', and possibly various others may play into the character—Goethe and doubting Thomas come to mind. I leave further speculations to the reader!

Maria

'In childlike natures such as that of Maria
there is a part that is free from the Luciferic taint,
and therefore it can be touched by the Christ.'

Harry Collison[1]

To transform The Beautiful Lily of Goethe's tale—a character so
perfect that literally no person can touch her—into the credible modern woman who is Maria, the 'leading lady' of the play, required
considerable dexterity on the part of the dramatist. The delightfully
complex interactions of Maria with the 'soul forces' of Philia, Astrid
and Luna and the relationship to her counterpart, The Other Maria,
are deftly presented. Maria is active in spirit: The Other Maria is
active in soul.

Maria is guide and mentor to Johannes as is established in the
first scene, in which she also presides as hostess. Whilst reliant on
the help and advice of Benedictus, she is clearly capable of taking
on responsibilities and is easily the most advanced of his pupils.
Throughout the drama it is the calming presence of Maria that reassures both Johannes and ourselves, the audience.

The first scene begins and ends with Maria listening to and con-
soling Johannes. His distress (and ours) is calmed by her entrance.
Scene three, in which Maria leaves her body, tests Johannes: he has
to rely on Benedictus. It is in the Devachan scene (scene seven), that
recognition of Maria affords him certainty of his spiritual vision.

Acting the Part

These three scenes prior to the Interlude pose great demands on the
actress. The usual control and equanimity of the highly developed
spiritual pupil is replaced in the third scene by one apparently hys-
terically possessed by 'the prince of hell'[2]. Steiner said of the revela-
tory conversation between Maria and the soul forces in scene seven
that it came directly from the spiritual world. He often enlisted the
services of Marie Steiner to present it in lectures in the speech and
drama courses. Marie Steiner was the extraordinarily gifted vehicle through whom Steiner was able to incarnate his inspirations and

innovations in the arts of eurythmy, speech and drama. Hans Pusch[3] tells us how uniquely adept she was and how difficult the part is for those following in her footsteps.

Maria's Mission

Benedictus, in scene three poetically describes Maria's character and upbringing. These have made her a suitable candidate to become a viable agent for the work of the Archangel Michael. He tells Maria:

> In many lives you had acquired
> an openness for the nobility
> alive in human hearts.[4]

He renders an illuminating description of her development—a development much in accordance with the principles of Steiner education. Everything has evolved in stages, in accordance with nature and spirit—nothing rushed, a natural process of growth.

We subsequently learn in the Devachan scene how advanced Maria was in a previous Hibernian incarnation—as messenger of Christ, she was calmly able to persuade the pagans that a higher power was working through their gods.

The Helper

Her problem is that those she tries to help—particularly Johannes and her child—regress rather than benefitting from her endeavours, and feel thwarted by her efforts. As with The Beautiful Lily of Goethe, her own level of perfection causes paralysis to those she seeks to help. Benedictus tells her:

> The spirit in you works
> in everything that can grow ripe in man
> as fruit for realms eternal.
> And therefore much it must destroy
> that only has its place within the realm of time.[5]

The ingratitude and depression suffered by those she seeks to help are the outward expression of the faults that have been pierced by the unerring arrows of Maria's higher self. This will, however painful at the present time, lead to great strides in future development:

> Its sacrifice in death, however,
> is seed of immortality.
> What flourishes for higher life
> must bloom from death of lower being.[6]

As Collison perceptively observes:[7]

> In childlike natures such as that
> of Maria, there is a part that is free
> from the Luciferic taint, and therefore
> it can be touched by the Christ.

The higher ego in Maria is building up the Spirit Self. The power of the Spirit Self in Maria destroys what is not yet purified in other souls—but in so doing strengthens them for future progress.

She has become the mother of the child through destiny rather than blood. When questioning Benedictus about her problematic influence on the child, she manages to remain calm and unemotional, although the child has aroused motherly instincts in her. She still asks the right question:

> Why do I ruin friend and child
> when lovingly I try to do for them
> the work that spirit guidance
> lets me perceive within my heart as good?[8]

Theodora reveals that the child was the one individual in the crowd of pagans of the Hibernian incarnation, opposed to the messenger of Christianity (Maria). This karma is playing into the present incarnation.

Her Special Destiny
The special destiny of Maria is revealed by Benedictus in the third scene. Her attributes and temperament warmly described by him have ensured that it is she who has been chosen as:

> that human being
> who might be worthy to accept within his soul
> the seed force of the god.[9]

Harry Collison elaborates on this:

> Maria has a special destiny. She is a chosen vessel for the
> Michael Spirit of the Age. Through her, Michael can work to
> develop the new spirit sight (waking clairvoyance in contrast to
> the atavistic trance). Michael can penetrate to the etheric and
> Maria is to carry over to the physical.[10]

This part of the play is difficult for the audience. We see,
apparently, Maria herself, cursing Benedictus. Rudolf Steiner
explained:

> The hierophant makes Maria aware that before she can fulfil
> her mission she must be influenced by a higher being. Con-
> sequently the higher members of her body separate from the
> lower and are possessed by a subordinate spirit. If you allow
> this scene to work on your soul, you can begin to see great
> mysteries in human evolution.[11]

Steiner reveals that:

> Whenever a person is chosen to serve a specific function in
> human evolution direct intervention by a divine spiritual being
> is required.[12]

Maria explains in the Devachan scene (scene seven) that far from
raging at Benedictus, she was exulting in joy and gratitude at her
mission. It is fruitful to juxtapose scenes three and seven and to read
them side by side, for example:

> You gave me clarity … that shrouded me in darkness (scene three).
> He gave me light … that granted me the power of sight (scene
> seven).[13]

Her lengthy and inspiring speech to Johannes in scene seven, herald-
ing the benediction of Benedictus upon their relationship, describes
and enlivens the strength of the bond between herself and Johannes.
In the Mystery Drama there is no embracing—the word shows their
level of attachment.

Maria's Appearances in the Final Scenes

Maria makes only four very short speeches in scene eight. Hers is the authoritative voice in the discussion about the spiritual inspirations fuelling Johannes's art. She tells Strader:

> One can pay tribute to the work
> without believing in its source.
> Yet in this case there would be nothing to admire,
> had not the artist trod the path
> that's led him to the spirit.[14]

This prompts Strader to the tirade of self-examination, which shows his pain in challenging his unbelief.

Her second contribution heralds Johannes's self-revelations in scene nine ('O man, unfold your being'):

> To find ourselves, we must unfold that power first,
> that penetrates into our inmost being.
> The word of wisdom says in truth:
> Evolve yourself in order to behold yourself.[15]

These lines surely hold the key to all anthroposophical teaching. Her third speech comments pertinently upon the development of Capesius and Strader:

> Capesius is closer far to spirit knowledge
> than he himself is yet aware,
> and Strader suffers deeply.
> His spirit cannot find
> what ardently his soul is looking for.[16]

She is a shrewd observer and her final speech prophesies astutely about Johannes's picture of Capesius:

> It will work further in that soul, for whom
> it pointed out the path into the spirit realm.[17]

In these brief comments we feel the reassurance of Maria's presence. Throughout the four dramas, we gain succour from her steadiness and equanimity. The turmoil of other characters shows us the travail and pitfalls of the anthroposophical path; Maria demonstrates the amazing vistas that open to us when we:

> unfold that power first
> that penetrates into our inmost being.[18]

In an even briefer appearance in scene nine, her reassuring presence brings the scene to a close, similarly to scene two. She is 'led there', and affirms the closeness of her relationship to Johannes:

> So closely are we linked
> that your soul's life
> lets its light shine into my soul.[19]

Her two speeches in the final scene are both addressed to Johannes, bringing the fairy-tale analogy with the Lily and the Prince to a close, and underlining her role as helper and guide to Johannes, which continues throughout the dramas.

Philia, Astrid and Luna

'Because they show themselves
so clearly in the Devachan scenes,
everything in it is alchemy in the
purest sense of the word. All of
alchemy is there—if one can
gradually discover it.'

Rudolf Steiner[1]

The metamorphosis of the three handmaidens of Lily in Goethe's tale into the individuals embodying the forces of the sentient soul (feeling), the mind or intellectual soul (thinking) and the consciousness soul (will forces), can surely be described as an alchemy of stagecraft. As they work within each of us in everyday life, such forces imperceptibly flow into one another. To clarify the process with the separation afforded by three individual characters on the stage, in front of our eyes, is a magical transformation unparalleled elsewhere in drama.

It would be very wrong, however, to regard the three as simply being representative types. Indeed their portrayal as ordinary, albeit perceptive, women in scene one, followed by the delightful, artistic interaction of their conversation with Maria in scene seven, clearly precludes Estella's criticisms of 'puppet-like types' in The Prologue. As Steiner tells us:[2]

> Should you ask, 'What are these three?', the answer would be, 'They are persons who are alive; they are Philia, Astrid and Luna—people. This always must be kept firmly in mind.

In Philia we see—and essentially, we hear—the qualities of the sentient soul with a primacy of the feeling realm. She is handmaiden of experience and faith or trust. The ether in which she operates is sound or chemical ether and, as we see in the Devachan scene, water is her element and the undines the nature spirits to which she refers.[3]

Astrid embodies sympathy and hope, positive qualities of the intellectual or mind soul. Her element is air; she operates in the light ether and is associated with the sylphs. The consciousness or spiritual soul informs the thoughts and deeds of Luna, who operates in the sphere of the will. Fire is her element, that of the salamanders, and hers is the life ether.

Certain attributes, too, are associated with them: strength and courage is the domain of Luna; love and self-sacrifice that of Astrid and change or metamorphosis is associated with Philia.

The three, who in scene seven become the 'handmaidens' of Maria, first appear as individuals in the initial scene. Philia is the first to speak, and her task is to spread soul-warmth to all. After remarking to Maria:

> Harmonious tones were there
> but also many a harsher dissonance.[4]

She subsequently gently admonishes Strader's 'dry prosaic reason', telling him:

> To speak of the unknowable
> may well allure the thinker
> but never human hearts.[5]

Luna speaks next to, 'Dear Doctor Strader'[6] and there is a clear affinity between Luna, Strader and Theodora. She admires the exertions of his will forces:

> And what you have described
> about your inner struggles
> lends weight to all your words—
> with even those
>   who cannot follow all you say.[7]

The will sphere of Luna connects to the karmic insights of Theodora and the strong will forces of Strader. Astrid is the third of the trio to dispute with him, before setting the scene for the entry of Felix and Felicia:

> The gleaming rays of sunlight
> that glisten in the morning dew,
> (*Felix Balde enters*)

the spring that gushes from the rocks,
the thunder rolling in the clouds,—
they speak to us in a spirit language.
I've sought to understand it.[8]

The person who can understand it is Felix, and Astrid's speech sets the tone of airy, natural beauty—the element pertaining to herself, Felix and Felicia.

Having briefly encountered them in the first scene, the audience suffers their absence until the Devachan scene (scene 7). The arresting tour de force of their conversation with Maria which opens this scene makes the wait worthwhile. The nine speeches concluded by the entry of Johannes are, in themselves, a poetic rhapsody in the Ancient Greek sense—part of a poem, ripe of itself for declamation.

Even in translation, the sublimity of this passage with its rhythmic interchange of gentle imperative from Maria and bounteous affirmations from the embodiments of the Michaelic beauties of her own soul forces nourishes those of the audience. She is here the Beautiful Lily of Goethe's tale and they are, 'the lovely maidens from the grove'[9], waiting upon her.

To add to the aesthetic delights of this interaction, there is, too, a strong element of teaching content:

> The speeches at the beginning of Scene Seven are a better description of sentient soul, intellectual soul and consciousness soul than any number of words otherwise would achieve.[10]

Steiner referred to this grouping of Maria and the three as an 'egoity' in which everything that Maria is supposed to be is distributed amongst her companions.

The interaction of the characters on stage, hopefully followed up by individual or group study of these sublime passages, affords us the possibility of at least a certain level of understanding of the cosmic mysteries embodied in these figures. They appear in each of the following dramas, along with 'The Other Philia', a counterpart of Philia in need of redemption. Their strategic use heightens and reinforces our awareness and understanding of the forces of the soul.

Their brief appearance in the final scene affords the 'egoity' of Maria to complete the healing process of Johannes who, we remember, remarked to Maria that her 'fire's noble force':

> robbed me of the interplay
> of my soul forces.[11]

Maria gives the initial reassurance, re-affirmed by the three in their usual appropriate order of utterance:

Maria: Johannes you have won in spirit realms
            knowledge now through me;
            to spirit knowledge you will add
            the soul's true being,
            when you can find your inmost soul
            as you found mine.

Philia: From out all world becoming shall
            the joy of soul reveal itself to you.

Astrid: With all your being you will now
            be able to illuminate the warmth of soul.

Luna: You may then dare to live yourself as Self
            when light can shine within your soul.[12]

The Other Maria

'You see in me the humbler sister only
of that high spirit being
who dwells within the realm
from which you have just come.'[1]

The Other Maria has an almost magical quality emanating from
the fact that her prototype is the Soul of Love. The fairy-tale aspect
of the first half of *The Portal of Initiation* charmingly accommo-
dates such a warm, gentle character. As the Green Snake in the
fairy tale, it is she who makes the crucial sacrifice—her life—for
the building of the bridge. In the play, her sacrifice is to join the
temple.

We meet her as an ordinary member of Benedictus's audience in
the first scene. Maria's description is almost befitting of the proletar-
ian heroine of a Ken Loach drama:

> She sacrificed her strength
> in bringing up her children carefully;
> her courage ebbed when early death
> took her beloved husband from her.
> In such a state, fate seemed to have in store
> a weary remnant only of her life.[2]

The Other Maria tells how finding Benedictus's circle has re-enliv-
ened her:

> The warm and magic power of words
> that here I listen to,
> streams down into my hands
> and flows through them
> like balsam …
> I do not ask the source of these words' power.[3]

This could be a description of the Mystery Drama itself—however,
from the standpoint of spiritual science, she should make such an

enquiry. She lives purely in the feeling realm. Her sacrifice is to turn to the wisdom of the temple:

> I must admit that noble purposes
> work blessing only in the light—
> and turn now to the temple.
> My feeling shall in future
> not rob the light of love of its effect.[4]

This is her only speech in the latter half of the drama. Dramatically her great contribution to the play is in scenes four and five in which she delightfully metamorphoses from the caring housewife of scene one to the 'mysterious nature figure',[5] who emerges from the rocks, covered in precious stones. Even in translation the sheer poetry of her initial utterance resonates:

> I wrest my way through rocky depths
> and seek to clothe the rocks' own will
> with human words;
> I sense the being of the earth
> and wish to think the earth's own thoughts
> within the human head;
> I drink in air of purest life
> and bring the powers of air
> transformed to human feeling.[6]

It is little wonder that the boyish, exuberant Wisp of the astral realm, Capesius, exclaims:

> I love your language, woman,
> and gladly would translate your kind of speech
> into my own.[7]

The fairy-tale plot is faithfully replicated in this scene as she, again with poetic language, informs the Wisps of the two available ways to the spirit world. In the fourth scene her speeches are preceded by a special melody, given by Steiner to the composer of music for the drama, Adolf Arenson, often played on the lyre or flute, enhancing the atmosphere of the 'mysterious nature figure'.[8]

The Humble Sister Only

Her relationship to Maria is that of 'the humble sister only'. This juxtaposition of the two 'Maria-forces'[9] is a masterly stroke of the dramatist. Steiner explains that the characters' names are far from arbitrary. In the two Marias, we see The Other Maria working purely through the soul forces, whilst Maria navigates the path of knowledge and cognition. Steiner warns us, however, not to take his characters as symbols—each is a real person in their own right.

Steiner informs us:

> The Other Maria, the mysterious nature figure, is revealed to Johannes Thomasius as the soul living below the ordinary conscious soul quite inaudibly and imperceptibly as long as man lives only in the physical world.[10]

Her dramatic entrance of scene four is similarly followed by that in scene five with Felix Balde. Romanus is speaking:

> In me the world-will feels
> That human beings are approaching
>
> *(Felix Balde appears in his earthly form*
> *The Other Maria in soul form out of the rock)*
>
> who uninitiate, can free the spirit
> from sense appearance.[11]

Their entrance and commitment to helping the temple is a key moment in the play, leading to the downfall of Retardus. They have previously followed the older paths of wisdom, but are now uniting with the progressive voices in the temple. The Other Maria perceives that Felix believes:

> the time has ended now
> in which we served existence on the earth,
> still uninitiated through wisdom's light.[12]

and clearly concurs with this sentiment.

The nature wisdom of The Other Maria in the scenes of the astral world and also in the speeches of Felix must now metamorphose into spiritual scientific cognition. As the Green Snake, her contribution to the drama is an essential one. Her sacrifice is vital. Johannes needs her movement towards the knowledge of the temple; he tells her:

> The sacrifice you bring the temple
> shall here be re-enacted in my soul.[13]

For Maria's development, the 'humble sister' had to 'come into the light'. This is articulated by Theodosius in the Sun Temple:

> Your destiny was closely linked
> unto your higher sister's life.
> I could bestow on her the light of love,
> but could not give the warmth of love
> as long as you continued to allow
> the best part in your nature to arise
> from darkness of your feeling only
> and did not strive to see it clearly
> with the full light of wisdom.
> The influence of the temple does not reach
> to motives rooted in blind instincts
> however much of good they wish to do.[14]

The need for wide-awake cognition is shown by the entry of Felix and The Other Maria into the temple. 'Darkness of your feeling', has to turn to the light of wisdom. Maria needed 'the warmth of love', to augment her own powers of cognition. The 'Maria-forces' in future dramas are manifest only in Maria herself; The Other Maria is absent from the other plays, having united her forces with her 'higher sister'. Her contribution to *The Portal of Initiation* not only facilitates the fairy-tale plot—the analogy with the Green Snake is a close one—but the alchemical, other worldly atmosphere of scenes four and five is in part conjured by her presence.

Capesius and Strader

'You must compel me
with your stunted weapons of dull thought
or you are nothing but
a fleeting phantom
of your own delusion.'

The Spirit of the Elements[1]

Capesius and Strader are derived from the 'Willow-o'-Wisps' in Goethe's fairy story. In the tale they are interchangeably mischievous—an ebullient double act, entertaining the reader with their insouciance, waylaying other characters, disrupting their plans and turning life upside-down. Unpredicted events in life, in which change is, often inconveniently, brought about by karmic necessity, perhaps—if handled well—advantageously, are personified in the Wisps.

It was a masterful stroke by Steiner to develop them into the clearly differentiated characters of the young Aristotelian, Strader, and the older Platonist, who is Capesius. Steiner informs us that in the Anthroposophical Society there is a mixture of Platonists and Aristotelians[2] now needing to work together, having in previous eras, incarnated separately. To be able to experience these temperamental differences through the juxtaposition of these two characters on stage helps us to understand something of the psychology of society members. This is fruitfully demonstrated throughout the four plays.

The Aristotelian, Strader, is more outward looking; Platonists direct their gaze inward. This is demonstrated on several occasions. One clear example is in scene four: when they are unsure how to proceed, Strader boldly proclaims:

> To follow the best way that we can find,
> with confidence, and use our caution,
> should lead us to our goal.[3]

Capesius conversely replies that they will find it by obeying, 'the impulse of our inner selves'.[4]

Their wispiness on the one hand, and their individuality, on the other provides a fascinating duality. In much of the first half of the play, particularly in scene four, they are the 'Will-o'-Wisps'. One may well suspect that Steiner enjoyed writing this aspect into their characters. The second half of the play loses the wispiness and develops their individuality as contemporary seekers of wisdom.

The first scene provides a forum in which this duality can thrive. They, as Wisps, forward sceptical arguments; Capesius can ridicule the revelations of Theodora and jovially sneer at Felix's way of speaking. Strader enjoys a strident, argumentative tone. They do, however, reveal doubts and vulnerabilities. Strader is moved by the revelation of Theodora and Capesius by the fairy stories of Felicia. We learn too of Strader's struggles away from 'the cloister' and Capesius's struggles with the dryness of knowledge[5]. We wait until their sojourn in the astral world (scene four) for wholesale wispiness to erupt.

Wisps in the Astral World
The fourth scene, in the astral world, poses a challenge to the actors. The ages of the Wisps are reversed; Capesius is a young man and Strader the elder. For an actor, such a change makes extra demands on the already stretched concentration: voice delivery and mannerisms must comply with the new chronological imperatives.

The youthful idealism of Capesius, who wishes to tell the world about the astral kingdom, has a boyish enthusiasm lacking in his now senior counterpart. The professor has, here, the warmth and energy of a petulant adolescent, and maintains his wispy cheekiness throughout the encounter with The Spirit of the Elements, who he insolently tells to:

> Seek reward
> wherever you can find it.[6]

Strader, in contrast, affects a more conscious coldness and arrogance to what he perceives as ignorance on the part of their erstwhile companion. He sneers:

> For the eternities, then, error and illusion
> would be what seems the truth

to man's best search for knowledge.[7]
(*lightning and thunder*)

The Spirit deftly replies and a short dialogue with Strader ensues in which, tellingly, the words of scene one, uttered by Strader himself, relating his vision of, 'a frightful, dream-born being of spirit darkness', are repeated by The Spirit of the Elements:

You must compel me
with your stunted weapons of dull thought,
or you are nothing but
a floating phantom of your own delusion.[8]

Strader's reply is defensive, but defiant. The following conversation with The Other Maria (the Green Snake), also follows fairly directly the narrative of the tale. The Wisps' reaction to The Other Maria is warmer than their attitudes to The Spirit of the Elements, although Strader maintains his haughtiness. He is, however, jolted by her presence—confronted by a being, or a fact:

But look—what a mysterious being!
It is as if the rock itself
had given birth to it.
From out what world foundations
do such things come?[9]

This question would seem to indicate that the words of The Spirit of the Elements:

Then it behoves you to acknowledge
that no man can know
from whence are gushing the sources of his thought
or where life's first foundations lie.[10]

are still echoing in Strader's mind. The dialogue with the Spirit is important for both Capesius and Strader, but does not immediately register with them. This whole scene in the astral world will subsequently gently resonate on a subconscious level with the Wisps. They will, however not clearly remember their experiences.

The dialogue with The Other Maria illustrates the contrast in the Aristotelian and Platonist temperaments. When she describes the first pathway to the spiritual world—the way of religious observance and self-sacrifice on which:

> You will soar forth in spirit wings
> toward primal origins of worlds.[11]

Strader immediately refutes this as 'fantastic'[12] and wants, 'to stay on the ground'.[13] After she describes the alternative route (through child-like, unknowing faith), Capesius replies that they are, 'thrown back upon ourselves' and need to:

> Work and to await with patience
> the fruits that ripen from our deeds.[14]

This is the stance of the inward-looking Platonist. In the astral world the wisps have caused thunder and lightning by their prosaic, materialistic utterances. This shows the audience in an extremely vivid manner how harmful such thoughts and words really are. Conventional wisdom has it that, 'sticks and stones may break my bones but words can never hurt me', but Steiner tells us that the way we think and the utterances in which we indulge do resonate in the spiritual world. The rumbling of the thunder and flashing of the lightning on stage imprints this idea more securely than simply hearing about it in a lecture.

The Wisps, in addition, have lumbered the unfortunate Felicia with the debt they owe to The Spirit of the Elements. Their appearances in the second half of the drama, which takes place after a gap of three years, are noticeably less wisp-like.

Character Development in the Final Scenes
The vision of Theodora has made Strader doubt his scepticism, and the doubt, which he dreads, manifests dramatically in scene eight. The picture of Capesius, resulting from the spiritual insights of Johannes and revealing aspects of the sitter's character unseen by Strader, who has known his friend some years, unnerves him. Doubt is Strader's enemy; his faith in science

which focuses only on the material world allows certainty—certainty is comfort.

Capesius, on the other hand, has benefitted from the fairy tales of Felicia, and was initially less inclined to the clarity of unbelief than Strader. He is content to acknowledge that Johannes's spiritual connectivity is informing the portrait. His enhanced understanding of spiritual development is revealed when he comforts the distraught Strader, who has 'lost the thinker's calm', at that very thought:

> Believe but good
> of such a moment.
> You had quite lost yourself,
> it seemed. The fact was, you were raised
> above yourself.[15]

Capesius understands the need to transcend earthly thought; Strader fears the consequences of so doing. Maria aptly sums up their predicament:

> Capesius is far closer to spirit knowledge
> than he himself is yet aware,
> and Strader suffers deeply.
> His spirit cannot find
> what ardently his soul is longing for.[16]

The attitude of either Wisp has shifted by the end of the play. What remains of their intransigence is now reserved for Retardus, who seeks to give them both a dressing down for their 'weakness' in not having 'driven out' the 'inclination towards spirit vision'[17] of Johannes and Maria. He gets short shrift; Capesius, the professor, courteously tells him, 'I never could convey your message rightly'. Strader, more bluntly, gives it to him straight from the shoulder:

> The weakness into which I had to fall
> is but the image of your own.[18]

Benedictus affirms that Capesius has now 'begun the path'[19] of spiritual development and can now build upon the foundation Felicia's tales have helped to form in his soul.

Strader is still beset by his adversary, doubt. The voice of Theodora yet again shakes this foe within him. She prophecies that he will in future say:

> I have now conquered for myself
> the power to reach the light.[20]

If Strader's doubt is not fully stifled, the audience surely has none.

Felix Balde

'I'm called a recluse and a dreamer
by those of kind intentions.
The others think of me
as just a blockhead
who all untaught by them
pursues his own poor nonsense.'

                                    Felix.[1]

Felix originates in 'The Old Man with a Lamp' in the tale—a wise individual whose lamp only shines in the presence of light from another source. He is a nature mystic able to express the secrets of the natural world in clear concepts, albeit in language incomprehensible (like that of the alchemists) to a contemporary academic such as Professor Capesius.

   His brief appearance in scene one with his wife, Felicia, establishes his almost obsessive enjoyment of solitude:

   I'm unaccustomed
   to mingle with so many people,
   and not just unaccustomed.[2]

The last line illustrates his inability to avoid speaking his mind. He is one of nature's own. His manner of speech is understood and lauded by Benedictus, but not for the scholar or the gentility of the tea room. His more gregarious wife complains:

   Ah yes, it is that way with him!
   It keeps us quite in loneliness.
   Year in, year out, we hear
   scarce more than what we speak ourselves.[3]

It is important for the dramatist to emphasize Felix's pleasure in isolation. We are being prepared for the crucial moment in scene five when his entry, with The Other Maria, into the Maya Temple, signals defeat for Retardus. His emergence from solitude and willingness to join the temple is essential for the advancement of Maria and Johannes. This emphasizes the need for anthroposophists to work together.

Felix embodies the Spirit of Nature and The Other Maria, the Soul of Love. Their joining the temple shows the need for the followers of Gnostic paths—nature mystics and those with Rosicrucian ideals—to navigate their way through into spiritual science.

Nature Wisdom

The affinity between Felix and Benedictus is established in the first scene when Benedictus enters as Felix is speaking. Such timing is always of significance in the Mystery Dramas. Felix self-deprecatingly demurs at Maria's relating that Benedictus has referred to, 'the hidden fount of wisdom in his friend'[4]. Benedictus crisply asserts:

> My friend you are mistaken
> Of untold value is for me each word of yours.[5]

This may call to mind the herb gatherer in Steiner's autobiography.[6] Enthusiastic research discovered his name was Felix Koguzki. Steiner says of him:

> He impressed one as if he, as a personality, were only the mouthpiece for a spirited content which sought for utterance out of hidden worlds.[7]

Of the way the real life Felix spoke, Steiner relates:

> One had first, in a certain sense, to learn his 'spiritual dialect'. To me also, he was at first unintelligible.[8]

One may, perhaps be reminded of how the intelligentsia treated William Blake when he spoke to them of his visions, when one sees the way that Capesius, the Wisp, mischievously refers to Felix as an 'odd stick' and disparages his wisdom:

> He speaks of sun-born beings
> that dwell within the stones,
> of moon-dark demons

who constantly disturb their work,
about the sense of number in the plants.
A listener will not for long
find any meaning whatsoever in his words.[9]

(Collison informs us: 'The gnomes associated with the solar forces build up the mineral kingdom. Dark powers, associated with the moon, fight against the powers of light in an endeavour to capture the gnomes and their kingdom.') [10]

We can see how true it is when Steiner refers to his characters as 'real people' and insists that he knew them. It is the spiritual dimensions of the drama which elevate it above the worldliness of ordinary 'realism', not fanciful flights of the imagination.

The Defeat of Retardus

The turning point in the defeat of Retardus arrives when Felix and The Other Maria enter the Astral Temple[11]. Just as the light of The Old Man with the Lamp cannot illuminate without the collaboration of another light source, the wisdom of Felix must unite with the temple. Retardus unsuspectingly tells his fellow hierophants:

As long as yet no mortals
have come into this place
who, uninitiate,
can set the spirit free
from sense reality,
so long am I permitted
to curb your eagerness.[12]

It is the entrance of the two unschooled repositories of the ancient sources of wisdom which signals his defeat.

The needs of the earth working through the will of Felix have propelled him into this sanctuary. Again we see the respect Benedictus shows him:

My friend, so let us hear
what you have learned within your inmost soul
about the bitter sorrow
in depths of earth.[13]

This allows Felix to launch into a vigorous critique of the superficiality of scientific ideas and the lack of depth in materialistic notions:

> For what evolves today
> within the brains of men
> can serve the surface of the earth,
> but does not penetrate the depths.[14]

His satire becomes quite waspish as he makes analogies with a merchant being offered money made of mist and sardonically denigrates a science which believes:

> that all untutored, void of spirit,
> the antediluvian animal
> could of itself become a man.[15]

The scene ends with the embodiments of the Spirit of Nature and the Soul of Love uniting with the three hierophants to ease out Retardus. Felix re-appears in the final scene. After a reprimand from Romanus for standing 'aloof a long time from the temple', [16] he characteristically candidly admits:

> It was men's very folly that from dark depths
> has shown to me the light
> and let me find my way into the temple.[17]

It is through the decisions of Felix and The Other Maria that Johannes and Maria have been able to free themselves for future development. As Retardus says:

> I see myself compelled now to
> relinquish both of them.[18]

Felix's Role in the Drama

Felix is only in three scenes, two of them very briefly. His part is, however, far from inconsequential. In scene five he contributes another angle to the discussion which continues throughout the play, pitting the insights of spiritual science against the limitations of positivistic ideas. His pithy angle on life contrasts intriguingly with the standpoints of the other characters. His relationship to The Other Maria and their entrance into the temple are significant in advancing the plot. His resolute isolation followed by the change of heart underlines the need for spiritual seekers to work and harmonize together. The need to listen to nature wisdom seems even more pertinent in our own time than it was when the play was written. Felix and his fairy-tale-telling wife are an odd couple, and as such much needed in the Mystery Dramas. They bring colour and vivacity to the group of seekers, and their own individual ways of expression and rustic spikiness adds grit to the language of the drama.

Felicia Balde

'They robbed my child
of all the forces of his soul,
and I should walk around
a monster in the sight of men,
that for them fruits may ripen
which bring but little good?'

Felicia.[1]

Felicia's equivalent in Goethe's tale is The Old Woman with the Basket, who struggles through the tribulations imposed on her by the Wisps and the Giant. The Old Woman is a more vulnerable victim—Steiner transmutes her into a character with greater wit, charm and vivacity. We cannot imagine Frau Balde falling for the flattery of the Wisps or being hoodwinked by the Giant.

Karmic Connections

It may seem strange that a worldly scholar such as Professor Capesius beats a retreat to the Baldes' cottage to hear fairy stories. Why should they have such a nourishing effect on his soul? This apparently inexplicable phenomenon shows us the strength of karmic forces. Capesius and Frau Balde have a strong karmic connection.[2] This allows her utterances to flow into the soul of Capesius and dispel the paralysis of dry, prosaic thought. One main task of the Mystery Dramas is that of a vivacious exploration of the quirks of karma.

Fairy Tales in the Mystery Dramas

The fact that Felicia is a metamorphosed fairy-tale character, who tells fairy tales herself, was a neat sleight of hand by Steiner. Felicia appears in all the plays. As we have seen, the dramas rely heavily on the word. The fairy tales of Felicia add an extra dimension to this process. Mantras, prayers, Socratic dialogues, incantations, lyricism and ritual—the more variety of utterance of a poetic and imaginative nature, the richer is the mixture. Felicia's lively, forthright manner of self-expression and her storytelling gift contribute well to the aesthetic.

In Steiner's time there was a greater general level of interest in fairy stories than is the case today. Folk traditions were explored in many countries. Folk songs were investigated by classical composers such as Bartok. Folk tales were collected by writers such as W.B.Yeats.[3] In Germany the work of the Brothers Grimm had a profound effect, arousing great interest in fairy tales. From an anthroposophical standpoint they open imaginative vistas and contain pearls of spiritual wisdom, often originating from past aeons. Storytelling features in the programmes of many anthroposophical institutions.

Felicia's storytelling is rooted in tradition, but she is developing an art that is dependent on new spiritual vision. The stories have a curative effect and can heal the spiritual aridity suffered by the Wisps. The power of art is referred to throughout the play—in the Prelude and the Interlude and through the characters of Johannes and Felicia.

Her Role in the Play

Felicia appears in only three scenes. She has just two short speeches in the opening scene, complaining of the Baldes' isolation, and referring to the visits of Capesius. In the final scene she rounds on Retardus and robustly asserts her confidence in her art:

> That men can kindle in themselves
> The fire for thought without your help,
> I've shown you clearly.
> There streams from me a knowledge
> That's able to bear fruit.[4]

It is only in scene six, however, that we are given evidence of her abilities. For the services he rendered to the Wisps, The Spirit of the Elements demands repayment from Felicia. This parallels the sequence in the fairy tale in which the Old Woman with the Basket has to pay the Ferryman three onions, three cabbages and three artichokes. Her hand becomes blackened and shrivelled, causing her, naturally, considerable upset as she prides herself on having beautiful hands. Similarly Felicia is threatened with 'ugliness of body'[5].

The vegetables in the tale relate to the parts of the plant—onions being roots, cabbages are leaves and artichokes are flowers. Collison tells us the nine represent the nine muses and 'Felicia's gift of creative phantasy points to the renascence of the arts as they receive life from spiritual knowledge'.[6]

The Woman in the tale and Felicia are both kindly—the Woman consoles the distraught Lily. Felicia, however, demonstrates strength and resilience in her dealings with Retardus, and her replies to The Spirit of the Elements. She is understandably upset at the idea of becoming ugly, but is generally calm and measured in her replies to the Spirit.

Felicia expresses both light and warmth. Hers is both the pure thought generated through the intellectual soul and the warmth of intuitive thought of the consciousness soul. Both Capesius and Strader are in need of the latter. Felicia has the wherewithal to help them.

The Spirit of the Elements requires her to tell a fairy tale to the 'beings who serve me in my work'[7]. They are the elemental beings. This may not seem much of a hardship, to one who loves storytelling; it is, however, a truly spiritual deed. Rudolf Steiner tells us, elsewhere, that by enlightened thought and feeling we release the elemental spirits trapped in the world of sense. The tale she tells, Steiner informed Collison, Felicia does not consciously understand. He also warned Collison 'not to read too much into it' or to 'add any fancy or imagery to it.'[8]

One needs, during the story, to remember that Felicia is telling it to the spirits of the rocks, in whose kingdom human love, hate and death play no role and would not be understood. It concerns:

> a Being
> that flew from East to West,
> following the journey of the sun.[9]

The Being observes human life with its love and its hatred. This did not cause him to stop as:

> hate and love create
> always the same a thousandfold.[10]

The Being did, however, leave his journey. He came upon an old man who:

> pondered over human love
> and pondered over human hate.[11]

And, feeling concerned for this individual, stayed with him a while before once more following the sun. We can imagine that Felicia's audience, the elementals, would be fully engaged with rapt attention, identifying with the pondering of the old man and the concern of the Being. The denouement of the story finds the gaze of the Being, during his journey following the sun, falling upon the dead old man, who has been released from his pondering. The elemental audience, listening with rapt attention, would, however, be rather shocked at this point. The drama and artistic impact are spoilt by Gairman's oafish attempt at satire.

This is then sternly met by Felicia:

> And who are you
> who thus distorts
> each word of mine
> in such uncalled-for manner?
> It sounds like mockery,
> and I am not the sort that likes to mock.[12]

Felicia is kindly, but does not like to be trifled with. She is strong in spirit. Her art is rooted in tradition, but she is developing an art that is also dependent on new spiritual vision. The stories have a therapeutic effect as has been shown by their effect on the Wisps, especially Capesius. The power of art is a leitmotif of the play, especially embodied in the characters of Felicia and Johannes.

Origins of the Character

The origins of the character are discussed in detail in an interesting article by David Wood in *New View* of Winter 2011/12. Her name, also that of her husband Felix, means 'fortune'. Wood cites Reinhold Köhler as the prototype for Felicia. Köhler was the head librarian in Weimar Library who had a vast knowledge of folklore and fairy stories. Steiner liked this amicable gentleman very much but an unfortunate incident occurred when Steiner requested a book. In trying to reach it on a high shelf, Köhler had a bad fall from which he never recovered. Steiner was very upset.

Köhler was the prototype for Felicia, but other contributors may include Goethe's mother, who nourished her son's imagination and creative powers with fairy tales. Wood also quotes the mother of Johann Wurth, whose son wrote, *The Diaries of an Austrian School-master*, a text which Steiner owned in his youth and from which he quoted enthusiastically.

Theodora

'But now the time draws near
when with new power of sight
the men on earth shall be endowed.
What once the senses could behold,
when Christ lived on the earth,
will be perceived by souls of men
when soon the time shall be fulfilled.'
                                        Theodora.[1]

Brief but Consequential Appearances

Theodora's appearances in the drama are brief, but impact heavily upon the play. The character originates in that of the Hawk in the tale—she can 'fly' forwards in her visions, as in the first and final scenes, and backwards as in the seventh. Each vision penetrates deeply the fabric of the plot.

The initial vision of Christ in the etheric is pivotal to all that follows in the four dramas. It occurs one third of the way through the first scene, avoiding the ugly symmetry of cutting through exactly half-way—Steiner's artistic sensitivity would disallow this. It is the only 'action' in that lengthy scene; its effect on the other characters, particularly Strader resonates strongly. Strader and Theodora's karmic interconnectedness is quickly established.

Theodora's visions set in train events and the understanding of karma. In dramatic terms, to use perhaps a trivial comparison, she is like the magical characters in fairy tales who move the plot onward—the fairy godmother promising, 'You shall go to the ball'. She helps to cement the partnership of Johannes and Maria by her revelation in scene seven, and to progress the relationship of Maria and her child. Her effect on Strader is a game-changer. She re-appears in the retrospect of the second play as Celia, as herself in the third play, and as a spirit in the fourth.

Clairvoyance

In the first scene, Maria, at Theodora's request, explains:

She felt one day as though transformed.[2]

and elsewhere was shunned through 'her peculiar nature'. The description Maria gives of how in visionary moments, which occur involuntarily, during which all else seems extinguished, seems to indicate that Theodora possesses the old, atavistic type of clairvoyance. Hutchins argues:

> Her character during the subsequent
> plays shows a poise and wisdom one
> does not associate with atavistic powers.[3]

There seems some truth in this, but, however one argues the case, the visions themselves are brought about in an unwilled manner through the subconscious. Maria points out:

> through our kind of thinking we become
> quite willing to accept unusual things.[4]

This is an important message to anthroposophists and others. Clearly Theodora has had a difficult time before finding Maria's group. Although Theodora emanates from the Hawk, there are also, perhaps, the positive elements of the Wisps—the irrational but beneficial aspects of life, associated with karma.

The first speech of Theodora occurs directly after that of Luna and confirms the latter's disquiet about the sceptical words of Strader. Theodora relates to Luna, who works in the will—the sphere of karma. The affinity to this realm also underpins her connection with Strader, to whom she listened with compassion—he also operates in the forces of the will.

In the third scene we find that Theodora has impacted on the relationship between Maria and the child. The child was attracted initially to Theodora, but, Maria informs us, when she was having a visionary experience, he saw:

> the glimmering light within her eyes.
> He felt his young soul shaken to the core
> and, frightened, rushed to me.[5]

The karmic ramifications of this are revealed in Theodora's vision in the Devachan scene. It is there that she tells that the child was the erstwhile opponent of the preacher (Maria) bringing Christianity to the pagans.

A Poetic Finale

Theodora's final speech is also visionary and provides a suitably poetic finale to the play. It is Strader, who in the final scene is still stricken with doubt. Theodora's reassurance anticipates their relationship in future plays and endows the drama with an inspiring and rousing climax of completion:

> Out of your heart
> soars up a glowing light.
> a human image
> shapes itself from it,
> and words I hear
> this human image speaking.
> And so they sound:
> 'I have now conquered for myself
> the power to read the light.'
> My friend, trust in yourself!
> For you yourself will speak these words
> when once your time shall be fulfilled.[6]

Demands on the Actor

The part, although not lengthy, makes stringent demands on the actor and requires delicacy and judgement. There is a clear, bright directness in her delivery—she is very far removed from a stereotypical mystic. All vagueness and feelings of olde-worlde sorcery are out of the question. As Hutchins indicates, Theodora has all her wits about her. Each dramatic revelation is preceded by the words, 'I am impelled to speak'. She is aware of the forces requiring these utterances. The following descriptions are crisp and cogent.

The Prototype and Other Contributors to the Character

In a fascinating *New View* article of Autumn 2013, David Wood suggests Mathilde Theodora Scholl as the possible main character source for Theodora. Scholl was a member of the Theosophical Society who, like Theodora had a profound spiritual experience. She became a pupil of Steiner's and in her book, *Der Weg nach Damaskas* referred to the Christ revelation.

Other possible contributors include the atavistic 'Seeress of Prevost', a certain Friedericke Hauffe referred to by Rudolf Steiner in connection with the history of spiritualism and the occult movement[7]. She was famed for her visions and biography, *The Seeress of Prevost*, by the medical doctor and author, Justinus Kerner. Madame Blavatsky is cited as are Helene von Schewitsch and Alice Sprengel.

Frau Schewitsch, who died in 1911, met Steiner in Munich, but remained loyal to Madam Blavatsky's teachings, trying to understand theosophy from a scientific perspective. Alice Sprengel was the actress who originally played Theodora and, herself, had visionary experiences. She suffered, however, from an unstable personality and came to have delusions of grandeur, believing herself to be the inspirational muse of Rudolf Steiner. She caused problems and had to be expelled from the Anthroposophical Society.

Benedictus

'There forms itself within this circle
a knot out of the threads
which karma spins in world becoming.'
                                      Benedictus.[1]

Benedictus is the spiritual teacher who guides Johannes, Maria, Capesius, Strader and others in the Mystery Dramas. His origins are as the character of the Golden King in Goethe's fairy tale. This king embodies wisdom and metamorphoses into the sure-footed, dependable spiritual counsellor and guide of the Mystery Drama.

Wisdom involves tactfulness and the sagacity to pose pertinent questions. The Golden King enquires of the Snake, 'What is grander than gold?'

'Light', is the answer.

'What is more refreshing than light?'

'Speech.'

To the Man with the Lamp he demands, 'How many secrets knowest thou?' which sets in train the action as the Snake whispers the fourth secret (her resolve to sacrifice herself).

Benedictus is similarly shrewd in his handling of discourse. His brief appearance in scene one, in which he gently informs Capesius of the nature wisdom of Felix, shows how he skilfully encouraged the latter to reveal his knowledge:

> *Felix:*   I only dared to speak
>   because you hid
>   how much you know yourself.[2]

This gift of being able to discreetly control situations without imposing on the liberty of others is particularly illustrated in scenes three and five, in which he listens attentively to others and gently ensures events go in the right direction.

In the third scene he listens to Maria, initially allowing her to take charge of the conversation, whilst subsequently, with Johannes, he knows it is incumbent upon himself to direct the proceedings.

Answering Maria's enquiries, he becomes a narrator, giving a charming description of her upbringing and eligibility for the special mission as a vehicle for the Michael Spirit, informing both her and the audience. He then has to help Johannes through the ordeal of Maria's body being occupied by Lucifer, 'the prince of hell'[3]. He gives Johannes the necessary confidence to find Maria in the spirit world:

> I can still further give you the direction:
> call forth the fiery power of your soul
> with words which uttered through my mouth,
> give you the key to spirit heights.[4]

Benedictus then gives the mantram/prayer/and answer, of which Collison informs us:

> These should be learnt in German for cosmic forces are contained in the very sounds of these words. They are 'redeemed words'.[5]

The English and German versions may be found in Appendix 2. Similarly the mantram at the conclusion of the Devachan scene (scene seven) may also be found in English and German.

The fifth scene sees Benedictus as the only hierophant fully awake—he is the progressive force of energy in the Maya Temple. Romanus and Theodosius are etheric haloes; they are representatives of traditions. Benedictus has to take the lead, but with tact and diplomacy. He tells his colleagues:

> My word springs forth from me alone.
> Through you the cosmic spirits sound.[6]

In Benedictus there is truly a harmony between the physical, astral and spiritual. He conducts the proceedings, but in a very restrained and refined manner. He stands back from the confrontation with Retardus, astutely letting Theodosius, Romanus, The Other Maria and, especially Felix, put the reactionary spirit firmly in his place. After The Other Maria's appeal to Felix:

> In union with the brothers who perform the rites
> within the temple, let us further work
> to bring forth fruits in human souls.[7]

Benedictus moves the proceedings forward:

> If you unite with us
> the work of consecration must succeed.
> The wisdom I have given to my son
> in him will blossom into power.[8]

Theodosius and Romanus then follow in step also with four-line speeches beginning, 'If you unite with us ...' and when Retardus asks, 'What will become of me?' Benedictus quietly and courteously insists:

> You will transform yourself to other life
> for you have done your work.[9]

The tenth scene features Benedictus speaking to Johannes in a calm and measured way, reminding him that he still needs help and guidance, but will progress if he stays within the auspices of the temple. The victory over Retardus is finalized in the last scene with his loss of Capesius and Strader.

Challenges for the Actor
The role is challenging for the actor. His contributions in the first and final scenes are brief, but scene three involves two lengthy narrations in taking control of a challenging scenario, scene five leading the Astral Temple, the closing speech of scene seven providing a climax to the first half of the drama, and brief but resonant appearances in scenes ten and the final scene. It is not an easy part to maintain. Benedictus lacks the eccentricities that often characterise charismatic teachers. It demands clarity and benevolent authority. Taking charge with gentleness and tact are not scene-stealers. Benedictus lacks the flamboyance of a Prospero. He cannot seem to be a magus, but with lengthy speeches he has to avoid dullness.

Not Steiner
He is always there for his pupils, knowing when he is needed, as was Rudolf Steiner, but Steiner categorically denied being the prototype for Benedictus. Dependable in matters esoteric though he is,

Benedictus clearly lacks many of the abilities and facets of Steiner. He does not seem to be a philosopher, or to be particularly interested in the arts. One cannot envisage him perched on a ladder carving 'The Representative of Humanity' or writing *The Philosophy of Freedom*. He does not spend time designing a building, discovering eurythmy, or writing a play. Was he, perhaps one of Steiner's own teachers?

Theodosius, Romanus and Retardus

'The power of love speaks thus
uniting worlds
and filling beings with reality.'
Theodosius.[1]

'My words are also not
the revelation of my being;
through me the world–will speaks.'
Romanus[2]

'You have been forced since earth's beginning
to suffer me within your midst.'
Retardus[3]

The metamorphosis of the somewhat mundane citizens, Theodosius and Romanus of the opening scene into the hierophants of the astral and Sun temples, with Theodosius becoming a mask for Lucifer in the penultimate station of the journey, is not only a masterpiece of dramatic stagecraft, but also a scenario which itself alone gives the audience much food for thought.

Retardus is portrayed only as a spirit and features in just the Astral Temple (scene five) and Sun Temple (scene 11). As a citizen, he would be a reactionary bore; as a representative of Lucifer he is judiciously substituted in the first scene by the vivacious and ravishing Helena. In Goethe's tale he features as the Mixed King, who collapses in a laughable heap, his gold having been sucked out by the Wisps. In the play, he is simply required to change:

Benedictus: You will transform yourself to other life
for you have done your work.[4]

Romanus and Theodosius represent outdated religious and mystical traditions—in the case of the latter degenerated into sensuous sentimentality. They are both archetypal figures and in scenes five and eleven, cosmic forces are speaking through these hierophants. The Spirit of Love speaks through Theodosius (the Silver King in the tale) and the Spirit of Action through Romanus (the Bronze King). This presents challenges for the actors, who are portraying two not overly inspiring earthly beings in the initial scene. Their voices have to convey a feeling of cosmic authority, which, however, should not be over-played.

Theodosius, in the first scene, argues well against Strader. His standpoint, however, is at a remove from that of spiritual science. He tells the anguished sceptic:

> This is the fate of those
> who only can approach the world through thinking.
> The spirit's voice, however, dwells within us.
> We have no power to penetrate the veil
> spread out before the senses
> and thought can bring us knowledge merely of
> the things
> that disappear in the course of time.[5]

This echoes the thinking of Immanuel Kant, who believed that the certainties of scientific knowledge were only available for matters pertaining to the five ordinary senses—all else was a matter of faith or conjecture. Steiner vigorously affirmed the abilities of spiritual science to investigate the higher realms.

Scene five sees the transformation which renders Romanus and Theodosius as etheric haloes. Benedictus's level of development and balance allows him to be fully present in the temple of the astral world in which the spiritual world of truth shines through, but a web of illusion is cast by the adversarial powers. The egos and astral bodies of Romanus and Theodosius are absent, thus ensuring they escape that negative influence of deception.

The Riddle of Romanus
Steiner explains[6] how it can be possible that such a prosaic, limited individual, as we see Romanus to be in the first scene, can possibly be the vehicle of the cosmic will. Romanus simply attributes the

achievements of The Other Maria to her good nature[7] ('her warm heart'). He relates:

> I cannot find the bridge
> that leads across
> from mere ideas to actual deeds.[8]

He is the kind of person who is thoroughly uncomfortable when conversation turns to spiritual matters. He roundly declares:

> When whirr of wheels
> is humming in my ears
> and when contented human hands
> are labouring at machines,
> it's then I feel the powers of life at work.[9]

Steiner suggests he may be a Marxist—more prevalent at the time the plays were written than is the case now—but he can surely be seen as representing a contemporary sensibility. From warehouse managers to those in charge of car dealerships, examples of such activity-driven, will-borne characters are numerous. But how did such an unpromising individual become the bearer of the cosmic will?

The Answer to the Riddle

Steiner explains with the analogy of seed and plant. Through his energy, determination and activity, Romanus is capable of much in the physical plane. He can be seen as a seed with great spiritual potential one day to develop. This portrayal is a timely warning to the audience against judgemental assumptions. Of such a person as Romanus he states:

> Here are the forces still latent in the seed, and they are good forces, important forces ... If you do not understand that a seed must be looked upon as the counterpart to such a person ... you will be experiencing the same kind of illusion as the one presented by the Subterranean temple.[10]

This duality of Theodosius and Romanus of individual/spiritual archetype lends an enigmatic fascination to these characters. It is less the literal meaning of their utterances that resonates, but the imagery surrounding it and the manner of their delivery. They are not simply representative types—they take on a life of their own.

The Final Scenes

The luciferic intrigue of scene ten, in which the duplicity spoken through the lips of Theodosius confounds both Johannes and the audience, burdens the actor with yet a third persona. Without giving the game away, there has to be a slightly airy, flighty quality as The Lord of Desire speaks through the mask of Theodosius.

The hierophants take their places in the Sun Temple scene, with Retardus and the coldness of doubt in the North, Theodosius, the Spirit of Love, in the warmth of the feeling realm in the South, Romanus, the Spirit of Action in the realm of the will in the West, and Benedictus in the East. The final scene is prophetic, a vision taking place in the soul of Maria. Potentialities have been realized and harmony achieved with the uniting of the streams.

The lengthiest contribution to the denouement is afforded to Retardus, whose complaints to Capesius and Strader are roundly derided by the latter:

> The weakness into which I had to fall
> is but the image of your own.[11]

Retardus continues to complain as to how the souls of Johannes and Maria now have to be relinquished and those too of Capesius and Strader (no longer Wisps). The vigour of his initial utterance:

> You've brought me into sore distress,[12]

becomes more of a lamentation by the end of the scene:

> Capesius, my son
> you are now lost.[13]

The affinity of Theodosius as the Spirit Of Love to The Other Maria is marked by his only two speeches in the scene expressing gratitude for her enabling him to endow the warmth of love to her 'higher sister'[14], Maria, having gently rebuked her for working from 'blind instinct'[15] instead of, 'the full light of wisdom'[16].

Similarly Romanus addresses Felix Balde who, 'stood aloof a long time from the temple'[16], but has now enabled Romanus:

> To illuminate the will
> of both Johannes and Maria.[17]

The ornate costumes of the hierophants add gravitas to this celebration of Michaelic wisdom.

We are relieved of the presence of Retardus in the succeeding plays. Theodosius and Romanus return in the retrospective in *The Soul's Probation*, as the first and second Master of Ceremonies. Theodosius becomes Albert Torquatus and Romanus is Friedrich Trautman in *The Guardian of the Threshold*. Romanus returns in *The Soul's Awakening*.

Lucifer and Ahriman

'Spirits desired
to cast a veil before the senses:
I tore the veil apart ...
I gave you your own will.'
Lucifer[1]

'Spirits desired
to rob you of the senses' beauty
in solid light.
I lead you onward
into essential truth.'
Ahriman[2]

The first stage appearance of the two forces of adversity was a daring landmark in the history of drama. They are absent from the fairy tale. One can, perhaps, reference the Mephistopheles of *Faust* as a precursor. Replacing this single entity with the duality of Lucifer and Ahriman creates challenges for director, actors and audience.

Their debut is carefully managed in gentle stages—two brief introductory speeches each in scene four, one each in scenes ten and eleven. They are, 'conceived as Soul-influences only'.[3] Lucifer, in the directions in Harry Collison's version[4], which would have been informed directly by Steiner, 'appears as female'. 'Lucifer has golden hair and wears crimson robes.' Ahriman, played by a male, 'has yellow robes'.

Whilst the Soul forces and the hierophants are clarified as human individuals in scene one and develop, taking on a life of their own, Lucifer and Ahriman are, of course, very different. It is challenging not to represent them as 'puppet-like types',[5] especially in the case of Ahriman.

They are 'the necessary forces of hindrance', replacing the dated binary pairings of good/evil and God/Devil, with the need for balance of the luciferic and the ahrimanic by the Christ force, as described in many Steiner lectures. Lucifer corrupts our inner life with yearnings and fantasies; he is the Lord of Desire. Ahriman wishes to immerse us in the deception of the primacy of matter; he is the Lord of Death.

Ahriman is represented in the first scene by the marble bust, stage left, reminding us of his presence, especially when spiritual seekers meet. Lucifer works through Helena, Christ through Theodora and Maria. The appearance of the two adverse forces in scene four, directly following the radiant mantra of Benedictus and the musing of the Spirit Voice, is poignant and dramatic, instantly changing the mood and atmosphere. For the dramatist in this play, they are like guns which threaten but do not fire.

Like two ogres, they pre-empt the more fairy-tale mood of the next few scenes. The separation of the two forces through our experience of them as vibrant entities on stage adds an extra dimension to our understanding of the nature of what may be referred to as 'evil'. To see it –literally—as such a polarity with the two figures enlivens what can be experienced conceptually to be a complex configuration.

In scene four, Ahriman, the Lord of Fear, seems to modify his pitch to entice the artist, Johannes:

> Spirits desired
> to rob you of the senses' beauty.
> I activate this beauty
> in solid light.[6]

He seems to be competing with Lucifer, the bringer of art. Lucifer claims to have given freedom to mankind; Ahriman responds:

> I lead you onward into essential truth.[7]

When recognized by Johannes, they instantly, surreptitiously disappear. Their entrances and exits are exquisitely timed for dramatic effect, in both scene four and scene ten. The mood alters as soon as they come—and as soon as they go.

In scene four, they address the lower ego of Johannes—the lower ego of the human being is a creation of Lucifer. Johannes has achieved recognition of his lower ego, but not of his higher self. The

tenth scene sees him deceived by Lucifer, working through Theodosius, who Johannes trusts, having seen him as a colleague of Benedictus—in the Maya Temple on the astral plane.

When Johannes, enthused by Theodosius/Lucifer conjures:

> You spirit, living in myself
> arise from your concealment
> and show yourself in your true being.[8]

in the expectation of the emanation of a glorious spirit being—the
re-entry of Lucifer, Lord of Desire, and His Satanic Majesty, Ahriman astounds and shocks both Johannes and the audience.

The composition of their speeches matches that of those of scene
four, but the content changes to reflect the enhanced maturity of
Johannes; the previous seduction attempts of each are replaced by
threats. The two introductory lines are inverted:[9]

	Scene Four:	**Scene Ten:**
Lucifer:	'O man, know yourself.'	'O man know me.'
	'O man, experience me.'	'O man sense yourself.'
Ahriman:	'O man, know me.'	'O man know yourself.'
	'O man, experience yourself.'	'O man sense me.'

Lucifer's promise, appealing to Johannes's initial naivety;

> And I could fill you
> with strength of selfhood
> self-being's joy.[10]

is replaced by the fear-inducing:

> You will find alien being
> in the wide regions of the heights.
> It will confine you
> to human fate.
> It will oppress you.[11]

Ahriman speaks not of 'bliss of revelation' but harshly insists:

> And you can squander
> in lofty light
> the strength of spirits.
> You can disintegrate.[12]

following which, the stage direction is, 'they disappear'. Harry Collison tell us that pupils seeking initiation must retain in their clairvoyant experiences a recollection of their earthly egos. This is facilitated by Ahriman. Lucifer preserves the ego in the earthly world (self-certainty) and if not for the ahrimanic beings who enable us to have memory, the human entity would fall apart in the cosmos.[13]

Scene eleven sees Benedictus allocating Lucifer and Ahriman to their rightful places in the background. They have to admit defeat as a result of the advancement of Johannes and Maria, but conclude their speeches with warnings of future involvement. It is Lucifer who provides a most resonant thought:

> The wisdom they have won
> gives them the power to perceive me.
> I only hold dominion over souls
> as long as they cannot behold me.[14]

Denial of the existence of the adversary powers allows them access. The configuration of Lucifer and Ahriman, being so much more nuanced and intricate than the old devil concept, required all the weaponry at Steiner's disposal to help us understand and work with these complexities. Lectures, mantras, the sculpture, 'The Representative of Humanity', and the stage portrayals in the Mystery Dramas are all needed for us to come to terms with their manipulations.

Gairman (or Germanus)

'I am the Spirit of the Earth-brain.
A dwarf-like copy of me
is all that lives in men.
Full many a thing is thought therein
which is but mockery of itself
when I reveal it in the size
which it takes on within my brain.'

Gairman.[1]

Gairman is certainly an intriguing character who strides the gap between the fairy tale (in which he mirrors The Giant) and the modernity of the play—in which he is a contemporary cynic, with mocking wit and a laconic, louche standpoint. We encounter him very briefly in the first scene in which he seems to have been impressed with the lecture and tells us that, in spite of himself he is getting hooked on what he is meeting in the group. Collison refers to Gairman as, 'a man with a hobby … occult research', and informs us, he represents the intellectual cynic, the destructive critic and the 'poseur'[2]. His initial speech expresses this frivolity:

> I've often lightly said in passing
> that I am fond of joking
> and only find in it some spirit,
> that for my brain it nonetheless
> remains a pleasant means to occupy the time
> between the hours of work and those of pleasure.[3]

However, although he may simply be placating his audience, he expresses some remorse and a wish to change. He continues:

> but this remark has now become to me distasteful.
> An unseen power has laid hold of me,
> and I have learned to feel
> what is much stronger in our human nature
> than the thin house of cards our wit sets up.[4]

In later plays he becomes Magnus Bellicosus. In spite of his significant name (all the names are significant in Steiner's plays), he rises
above purely selfish preoccupations and takes an interest in those
around him.

The transposition of The Giant in the fairy tale to the Spirit of
the Earth-Brain is appropriate. The Giant is weak, but in possession
of subconscious forces as is the case with Gairman in scene six,
his only other appearance in the play. Just as the Wisps are much
wispier in the astral world than on earth, Gairman's behaviour as
The Spirit of the Earth-Brain is similarly distorted. The forces of
The Giant are inherent in his shadow and used to cross the river
at twilight. These are the forces which can gatecrash the spiritual
world without needing the power of full consciousness—narcotics,
hypnotism, atavistic clairvoyance etc. The Giant steals one of each
of the vegetables that the Woman with the Basket is taking to pay
the Ferryman.

This action is closely paralleled in scene six of the play by the
gauche behaviour of Gairman, The Spirit of the Earth-Brain, when
he intrudes on Felicia's telling of the fairy story to the elementals.
The Spirit of the Earth-Brain is associated with the seventh stratum
of the earth. In the seventh sphere above the earth reside the spiritual archetypes of our moral qualities. Conversely, these are grossly
distorted in their counterpart beneath the surface of the earth. The
Earth-Brain,

> thinks thoughts on quite a different scale from those
> appearing on the small human brain. A man will often
> assert something he does not see in his own brain, but it
> will look grotesque when it is reflected in the giant Earth-
> brain.[5]

This distortion allows us to see the caprice, superficiality and
even outright banality of individuals. Through the Spirit of the
Earth-Brain, Gairman is propelled by those forces which prompt
The Giant in the tale to take the vegetables. The poetry of Felicia's tale and the imagery of the philosophical old man attract
Gairman, who in the astral world comes to more closely relate
to his prototype, 'The Spirit of the Earth-brain'. His mocking

pastiche of Felicia's tale is clearly quite uncalled-for and grates on her creative sensibility. Steiner says of The Spirit of the Earth-brain:

> Ridicule has to be a concern of his because he finds so much to laugh at in what human beings do.[6]

Gairman disappears from the play, just as The Giant in the tale metamorphoses into a 'colossal statue of reddish, glistening stone'.[7] His shadow points to the hours, 'not in numbers but in noble, expressive emblems'.[8] The forces of The Giant are productive when used in full consciousness.

The Spirit of the Elements

The Spirit of the Elements is,

> The Being who guides the incarnating soul into earthly life, and the sleeping soul back into the physical world[2].

He is the Ferryman in the fairy tale who takes the cantankerous Wisps across the river from the spirit land into the material realm. He derives from Charon, the ferryman in Greek mythology, who ferries people across the river of time, the River Styx, into incarnation and on the return journey after death. He only appears in scenes four and six and is absent from the following dramas.

The Spirit of the Elements shows himself to be a stern but kindly and benevolent figure. He understands the deficiencies of spiritual vision currently inherent in human beings:

> The human soul beholds me only
> when services I render him are over.
> Yet he obeys my powers
> throughout all courses of time.[3]

The Spirit is 'aged and stands upon a sphere'[4]. The fairy-tale element prevails in these two scenes and the audience is lifted by the nature-spirit presences of both The Spirit of the Elements and The Other Maria, who is 'dressed like a spirit … but one associated with rocks and precious stones'.[5] The Spirit has had considerable difficulty in bringing the Wisps out of the subterranean depths to the surface of the earth:

> The spirits and the elements
> arose in raging storm,
> when I was forced to enter

their kingdom with your beings.
Your kind of thought resisted
the ruling of my power.[6]

These lines form the crux of the brief but poignant Socratic-style dialogue he has with the Wisps, mirroring that of scene one in which they are similarly confronted by the pupils of Benedictus. The Spirit is calm and matter-of-fact throughout; his wisdom shines through in contrast to the effects of the sentiments expressed by the youthful Capesius and the aged Strader.

This part of scene four corresponds to the misbehaviour of the Wisps to the Ferryman. The Spirit rattles Strader by reiterating the very words the latter himself used in scene one:

You must compel me
with your stunted weapons of dull thought,
or you are nothing but
a fleeting phantom of your own delusion.[7]

Strader refers to these as 'terrifying words'.[8] His certainty has been shaken. The disappearance of the Spirit leaves Capesius and Strader in a quandary as to where to go. Like the Ferryman he knows he will be repaid!

As Lord of the Nature Spirits, he is the inspirer of Felix and Felicia Balde. When Felicia is summoned by him to repay the debt of Capesius and Strader, he is necessarily unyielding to her justified pleas of only having done good deeds to the unwitting Wisps who have inadvertently damaged her son with their positivistic ideas. He gently explains that it is a spiritual law that she must repay the debt:

It must be so.
Since you have served
the earthly part in them,
the spirit now demands through me
that you complete the work.[9]

The task he commands her to do—telling a fairy story to the elemental beings—hardly seems arduous for one who loves telling fairy stories. After the tale, he simply disappears, unnoticed as in life.

The Seal

The lettering gives us, moving in an anti-clockwise direction from the E and concluding with the central SSR, the initials of the Rosicrucian mantra:

Ex Deo Nascimur (Out of God we are born)

In Christo Morimur (In Christ we die)

Per Spiritum Sanctum Reviviscimus (Through the Holy Spirit we are reborn)

The threefold process of the mantra is seen in combination with the breathing process of the inner and outer designs. The outer and inner designs are each sevenfold. The mantra affirms the affinity with the Trinity. The twofold design of in-breathing and exhaling affirms the need to receive the spiritual as revealed through the world of nature in an outward gesture and to meditate inwardly.

Appendix 1: Goethe's Fairy Tale, The Green Snake and the Beautiful Lily

A glimpse at Goethe's life up to the moment he wrote his fairy tale

by Tom Raines[1]

A true fairy story is a work of art. At Michaelmas, in 1795, there appeared in the German magazine *Die Horen* (The Hours) a series of stories of which the concluding one was a Fairy Tale, *The Green Snake and the Beautiful Lily*. This tale tells of magical transformation, yet one which, when the time is ripe, can be experienced by every human being. The author of these stories was Johann Wolfgang von Goethe and the creation of this Fairy Tale was to have far reaching consequences. Who was this Man and what was the significance of his Fairy Tale?

This introduction to the Fairy Tale and its creator, brief though it is—for one could surely write a whole book and still leave much unsaid—offers the reader a broad sketch of Goethe's life as it unfolded up until the moment he committed his tale to the written word. This gives us some ground upon which to stand as we look together at how the Fairy Tale came to be created, following a little of its destiny in the world and seeking what might be its relevance for us in our time.

Goethe entered the world on 28 August, 1749 in Frankfurt am Main, Germany. He was destined to become a giant in the cultural life of Europe, producing a truly astounding body of work during the course of his 82 years of life on earth. Goethe's contribution to world literature is universally acknowledged, the breadth and depth of which in its wisdom has often been termed 'Olympian'.

His creative work and interests encompassed many areas and disciplines, including those of critic, journalist, painter, theatre manager, educationalist and natural philosopher. He produced prose and poetry across a variety of themes, displaying a command of many styles, whilst never losing the power to produce magical, short lyrics wherein he made the manifold mystery of human existence transparent. His creative faculties remained remarkably intact to the end of his life, epitomised by his masterpiece, *Faust,* that he worked on and developed for 60 years, completing it just before his death on 23 March, 1832.

Goethe was also a natural scientist and his writings in this field alone produced some 14 volumes. He recognized that in observing natural processes, like a growing plant, a large part of the process of such a living organism's 'coming into being' is invisible to our normal senses. A contemporary of Goethe's, born some six years before him, was the philosopher Kant, whose ideas still stand behind much of our modern thinking. It was Kant who stated that the type of intelligence necessary to know these hidden processes in organic nature would be an intuitive intellect—*intellectus archetypus*—that, Kant asserted, was beyond the capacity of humankind. Nature, when revealed, manifests both the truth of scientific knowledge and the beauty of the creative act. But these were separate for Kant: science was separated from art. Goethe, however, brought art into his approach to science and made of them a unity. He did an enormous research work on how to observe Nature and in so doing brought a new approach to natural science. He was both a student and a 'revealer' in artistic form, of the secrets of inner human nature and the outer manifestations of 'Mother' nature. His own experiences showed him that through a willingness to observe with the senses, free of any preconceptions, deepening this process to the point of becoming aware of one's inner responses, then one could come to an intuitive knowing of Nature's hidden processes. He held the conviction that both art and science led to, and sprang from, the 'primal source of all being' out of which came the whole of creation. His Fairy Tale belongs to this source.

Born into a middle-class family of cultured parents, Goethe received a wide and rich education. His father was a retired lawyer from the North of Germany. His mother, the daughter of a Mayor of Frankfurt, was able, in time, to open up many connections for her son with the dignitaries of that city. At the age of 17, Goethe would have preferred to have read classics at the then newly founded University of Göttingen where the influence of English prevailed, but instead, he followed in his father's footsteps for a moment by going to study law at the University of Leipzig.

A few years later, in July 1768, he awoke one night in a desperate state; his lungs were haemorrhaging. He suffered an enormous loss of blood and nearly died. A long period of recuperation followed and for the next two years he was cared for at his Frankfurt home by Susanna Katarina von Klettenberg, a friend and distant relative of his mother.

Susanna von Klettenberg was a mystic with deep spiritual perception and was a member of the *Herrenhuter*, the Moravian Church. This was a religious movement having its roots in the fifteenth century *UnitasFratrum* (Unity of Brethren or Brothers) Hussite movement of Bohemia and Moravia. This woman had realized that this near-death experience was a turning point in the young Goethe's life. As well as caring for his physical needs, she guided him into an awareness of spiritual realms of which he had been previously unaware. She brought him into contact with many written works on mystical subjects, especially books on alchemy by such men as Paracelsus, BasiliusValentinus and Franciscus Mercurius van Helmont. She had a friend, also a member of the *Herrenhuter*, a physician and alchemist called Dr Johann Friedrich Metz, under whose care and unique medicinal remedies Goethe slowly recovered. The deeper background of alchemy is connected to the Rosicrucians, those people who serve the aims of the individuality known as Christian Rosencreuz, who seeks to further the work of The Christ by transforming and spiritualizing the Human Soul and the Earth. Through his life-threatening illness, Goethe was brought into connection with the knowledge of the Rosicrucians and out of this influence and inspiration he was eventually to create his Fairy Tale.

Following his recuperation, Goethe transferred his studies to the University of Strasbourg where he developed a deep interest in natural science, history and folklore. He was now very active with his poetry and from this period came some of his finest lyric poems. Susanna von Klettenberg died in 1774 and Goethe was to later write a moving tribute to her *Bekenntnisse einer schonen Seele (The Confessions of a Beautiful Soul)* that he included in his novel *Wilhelm Meister.* That same year, Goethe had a meeting in Frankfurt with Karl August, Duke of Sachse-Weimar, a man who was to play a great role in his life. Eight years younger than Goethe, Karl August invited him to come to the city of Weimar and act as his personal advisor and counsellor. Initially Goethe agreed to come for only a few months, but this was to become his home for the rest of his life. Here Goethe took up ever-increasing responsibilities on behalf of the Duke and the affairs of State. This often involved extensive correspondence, interviews, conferences, travel and social obligations. One of the duties he was called upon to perform was that of Inspector of Mines and this took him to Illmenau, a few miles away from Weimar. Here, he became deeply interested in geology and mining principles. Through this work, coupled with the fact that Goethe's official residence was a *Gartenhaus* (Garden House) in a park on the edge of Weimar, we can perhaps see how this man's lively interest would be stimulated by the abundant plant and mineral forms with which he was coming more and more into contact. This interest would have been further supported by the proximity of the Thuringian forests and the herbalists he would often meet in the woodland countryside. Yet, all these duties were placing an increasing burden on Goethe, leaving less and less time for his own creative work, for he was now also director of the Weimar Theatre and was expected to write new plays as well as supervise stage productions. Finally, desperate for a release, he slipped quietly away for an extended visit to Italy in 1786. This was to last for over two years.

This journey to Italy had a profound effect on Goethe. The architecture, sculptings and paintings he discovered, influenced by the Greek, Roman and Italian cultures, drew forth many deep observations and insights from his soul. In the diary Goethe kept of this journey, he made the following entry under 6 September 1787: '... Supreme works of art, like the most sublime products of Nature, are created by man in conformity with true and natural law. All that is arbitrary, all that is invented, collapses: there is Necessity, there is God'. Goethe began to observe nature in a new and creative way. His faculty of observation, of 'seeing' ever more deeply into natural phenomena, was unfolding more and more and Nature began to reveal her secrets to him. In the botanical garden at Padua, whilst looking at a 'Fan' Palm tree, Goethe realized the importance of the *leaf-form*, showing itself in various stages of metamorphosis in a plant. This discovery worked further in Goethe, until, later in his journey, when he was in Sicily visiting the botanical garden of Palermo, it culminated in his receiving the profound experience of 'seeing' with his inner eye the *'Urpflanze'*—the 'archetypal plant'—the creative form behind all plant life. A new approach to science was now developing within Goethe, whereby he observed not only what was the phenomenon before him, but also what inner activity was called forth in him in those moments. Goethe conceived science as a path of inner development, where, by means of intensifying the sensory observation, the inner faculties of imagination, inspiration and intuition could come alive, enabling one to break through to a spiritual understanding of what was at the very root and heart of the natural world and its manifold manifestations. He felt that science should have as its highest goal the arousal of wonder through contemplative observation in which the scientist would come to see 'God in Nature and Nature in God'. Goethe wanted to open the eyes of the observer to what was spiritually at work in nature. His was a voice speaking over two hundred years ago, and yet his approach seems pressingly relevant today. It could be argued that the ecological crisis facing the modern world is really a crisis of our *relationship* to nature. The problem we face is not the degradation of nature, but rather the degradation of our *awareness* of nature. Many people today do not know how to look more deeply into nature for themselves, feeling that this must be the preserve of scientific 'experts', yet Goethe saw the human being as 'the most powerful and exact instrument if we but take the trouble sufficiently to refine our sensibilities'.

The events, the artistic and natural impressions which gave rise to so many insights during his Italian journey, Goethe recreated as a book, the reading of which clearly reveals how some of the experiences he made in Italy later became metamorphosed into aspects of his Fairy Tale. Goethe's scientific approach to observing nature is one that can also be applied to the reading of his Fairy Tale. If we recreate his word pictures in our imagination, we can observe them with the 'inner eye' and allow what they may reveal to speak to us.

On his return to Weimar, a loneliness descended upon Goethe as he discovered that few understood his newly awakened scientific awareness, preferring to admire only his poems and written stories. Nevertheless, he chose to plunge deeper into his scientific studies. These efforts bore an early fruit with the publication in 1790 of the *Metamorphosis of the Plant*. Here, Goethe followed the plant through archetypal stages of alternating expansion and contraction. He saw the leaf as the constant underlying form in the plant that was metamorphosed forwards and backwards (if we imagine the leaf as central in the plant between root/stem and flower), appearing in different forms as root, stem, leaf, bud, flower and fruit, or seed. He followed this a year later with the publication of his first essay on optics, which led to his monumental study of colour phenomena, *Zur Farbenlehre* (*Theory of Colour*, eventually published in 1810). Here, Goethe challenged the theories of Newton that sought to explain the phenomenon of colour in terms of the measurable angles of refrangibility of colourless rays of light, thus reducing the phenomenon of colour to a dead mechanism. Goethe's approach was to try and understand colour in its own terms as he experienced it arising out of the meeting of light and darkness in nature. He saw colour as the 'deeds and sufferings of light' as it manifested itself on the material plane. He treated it as something living. It is a qualitative approach that has always appealed more to artists than to scientists. J. W. Turner, the English artist and contemporary of Goethe, experimented at the end of his life with Goethe's theories and in the process painted some masterpieces.

Goethe came to recognize three principles at work in organic nature: metamorphosis, polarity and enhancement. In other words: changing of form, the meeting of opposites (for example, day and night) and a climax or 'crowning glory' in a piece of creation (like a flower on top of a plant). It is just these qualities of magical change, meeting of opposites and glorious moments of achievement, of fulfilment, that one finds in a Fairy Tale! When we bear this in mind, Goethe's life-path of development as a natural scientist—bringing his art into science and his science into art—becomes more visibly relevant to his ability to create a true Fairy Tale.

We have touched upon two occasions in Goethe's life when inner soul changes occurred, signalled by outer circumstances. Around the age of 18 he had a life-threatening illness and was led to a spiritual perspective of life through a person deeply connected to the Rosicrucian stream. Around the age of 37 he took an extended journey to Italy and deepened his faculty of observation, beginning to see Nature more with his 'inner eye'. Art and a new science open out for Goethe. These were times in his life when something happened which shaped his destiny, where he was able to take hold of new forces on his life's path. These moments occurred around the 'lunar node' periods of Goethe's life. What is this cosmic measure, the lunar node?

Briefly, viewed from the Earth, the orbits of the Sun and Moon are inclined at an angle to one another and intersect in two places. When the Moon is physically at one of these two intersecting points, and at the same moment is in a straight line with the Earth and Sun, this is called a lunar node. This special alignment occurs approximately every 19 years (18 years, 7 months, 11 days to be more exact). When a person is born, their body, soul and spirit unite on the earth. Ancient wisdom connected Earth, Moon and Sun with body, soul and spirit and so a person's birth was understood as a moment when the different aspects of these three heavenly bodies were in a spiritual 'alignment'. Of course the physical astronomical alignment does not occur with each person's birth, but its recurring *rhythm* of approximately 19 years was seen as applicable to every human birth, repeating itself throughout a person's life. The moment of birth is the moment we take up the journey of our earthly destiny, and the occurrence through our life of our lunar nodes can be seen as moments that can reveal something of our destiny in a special way, when seemingly outer events appear to shape something of our lives. For Goethe, the first repeat of his lunar node came at the time of his illness and the second occurred during his Italian journey. Occult knowledge of the stars offers the picture that around each time the rhythm of the lunar node occurs in a person's life, something of their true earthly destiny shines strongly into their life, illuminating and quickening it. This seems unmistakable in Goethe's life.

In the spring of 1794, Goethe travelled to listen to a lecture in Jena and afterwards, on the steps outside the building where the lecture had been given, he shared with the philosopher Schiller his experience of the archetypal plant. Schiller responded to Goethe's words by saying, 'That is not a description of something objective, but is only an idea.' To this Goethe replied 'Then it is clear that I see my *ideas* with my eyes.' This conversation was to mark the beginning of a wonderful and fruitful friendship, where both found enormous stimulation through each other's ideas. This relationship surely helped to alleviate the sense of loneliness that Goethe felt, for in Schiller he had found a kindred spirit with whom he could share his natural-scientific ideas.

Later that year Schiller proposed the publishing of a literary periodical to be called *Die Horen* and asked Goethe if he would like to contribute. Goethe was enthusiastic and as his first contribution offered a series of stories grouped together under the title *Unterhaltungen deutscher Ausgewanderteen (Conversations with German Emigrants)*.

These stories grew as a response to the times in which they were written. Goethe was born and raised during the period when the French movement of 'Enlightenment' brought rationalism strongly into European thinking. This one-sided intellectual thinking was a ferment for the subsequent French Revolution at the end of the eighteenth century. It is clear that Goethe was no rationalist and the waves breaking over his soul at this time as a consequence of events stemming from this way of thinking became a deep burden for him. Two years before, Louis XVI, the King of France, had been executed and now in 1794 the revolution was at its height and thousands of refugees were fleeing for their lives before the armies of France. Goethe took these events as the background for his series of stories for *Die Horen*. In them he had a group of dispossessed and exiled aristocrats wondering and fearing about the future. They represented, in their various characters, something of a cross section of humanity. Tensions built up between them and in order to help maintain a peaceful existence together it was suggested that, taking it in turns, on each evening one person should tell a story to the group, to give a little common ground to their small community and help raise their spirits. And so Goethe weaves six tales. Finally an old clergyman in the group proposes he relates the seventh and last tale to be told, which will be a Fairy Tale. He says, quite enigmatically, that it will remind them of 'everything and nothing'. Through the character of the old clergyman Goethe introduces *The Fairy Tale of the Green Snake and the Beautiful Lily*. In the context of the *Conversations with German Emigrants* it is totally different in style and content to the proceeding six tales and clearly stands as a tale by itself.

This Fairy Tale was written by Goethe as a response to a work of Schiller's entitled *Über die aesthetische Erziehung des*

Menschen (Letters on the Aesthetic Education of Man). One of the main thoughts considered in these 'letters' centred around the question of human freedom. What should be the condition of the human soul forces to achieve this freedom? Schiller recognized Necessity (instinct, passion, the realm of the Senses) and Reason as two forces in the human soul. If either one predominated over the other, it prevented the human being from attaining real freedom; either the soul would be driven by blind necessity, or else a cold reason would suppress all passion and instinct. Only by establishing a middle ground, where necessity and reason harmonized, could freedom exist. Thus Schiller had conceived of a threefold model of the human being, where, in the balance between the two poles of Necessity and Reason, Freedom would exist for the Human Personality. Schiller saw that a harmonious social life could only be founded on the basis of free human personalities. He saw that there was an 'ideal human being' within everyone and the challenge was to bring the outer life experiences into harmony with this 'ideal'. Then the human being would lead a truly worthy existence. Schiller was trying to build an inner bridge between the Person in the immediate reality and the 'ideal human being'. He wrote these 'Letters' during the time and context of the French Revolution. This revolution was driven by a desire for *outer* social changes to enable human personalities to become free. But both Schiller and Goethe recognized that freedom cannot be 'imposed' from the outside but must arise from *within* each person. Whilst he had an artistic nature, Schiller was more at home in the realm of philosophic thoughts and although Goethe found much pleasure in these 'Letters' of Schiller, he felt that the approach concerning the forces in the soul was too simply stated and, it should be said, working in abstract ideas was not Goethe's way. So he set about writing a Fairy Tale that would show, in imaginative pictures, the way in which a human soul could become whole and free, thereby giving rise to a new and free human community. And this was published in *Die Horen* in 1795. Goethe's life continued, encompassing many notable experiences and achievements but we will let his biography rest here, for we have arrived at the moment of birth of *The Green Snake and the Beautiful Lily* through his creative hands.

Goethe lived in a moment of history that carried profound inspirations on its breath. Between the Rationalist period of European thinking and the beginning of scientific materialism around the third decade of the nineteenth century (about the time of Goethe's death), there happened a most creative period of human thinking and consciousness. This was the moment known as the Classical period in Germany that was followed by a brief flowering of Romanticism all over Europe through such people as William Blake in England, with his prophetic art and poetry, and Novalis in Germany who brought through his poetry and other writings a spiritual interpretation of Cosmos, Humanity and Earth. Goethe was perhaps the most prominent representative of this movement, who, with his contemporaries, stood in the world for a moment, united by their endeavours to open a new thinking for a new knowledge, vouchsafing the future development of humanity. When this wave of spiritual endeavour receded under the pressure of scientific materialism, its achievements looked to a future time for a deeper unfolding. Are we now ripe for this in the twenty-first century? Could we say for ourselves, 'The time has come'?

This cry, 'The Time has Come!', rings throughout Goethe's Fairy Tale, which is set in a landscape divided by a river. This acts as a boundary between two lands, that of our normal 'daytime' consciousness and that which is not accessible to our normal sense perception—The Land of the Senses and the Land of the Spirit. By the end of the Fairy Tale, there is a permanent bridge spanning this river, joining these two Lands together. The theme of love and sacrifice bringing about a true and harmonious community emerges as the tale unfolds. Many magical and seemingly illogical happenings occur, as is the way with any true Fairy Tale because they have their own laws at work within them. These are not understandable through the rationale of our normal intellectual logic, rather it is a higher spiritual 'logic' that is at work. Goethe's understanding of the three principles in nature of metamorphosis, polarity and enhancement—or moment of climax—do not seem out of place in approaching this 'higher logic'. A number of different characters appear in his Fairy Tale, interacting with one another, weaving together towards a climax that is experienced with the marriage between the Beautiful Lily and her Prince and the joining together, by means of the bridge, of the two Lands. The one event is dependent and linked to the other.

The Fairy Tale begins with a Ferryman, asleep, who lives in a small hut by the river. It is midnight and he is woken up by two

Will o' the Wisps, gentlemen seemingly made of flames of light, and asked to take them across the river. This he does. But, the Ferryman can only take passengers in this direction, none can return with him from the other side. Later, we realize that they are crossing over from the Land of the Spirit to the Land of the Senses. Soon there is a meeting with a Green Snake. She lives in a chasm in the rocks and has access to an underground chamber which is later revealed to be a temple containing four Kings; one each of Gold, Silver, Bronze and the fourth a mixture of all three. The Will o' the Wisps devour gold wherever they find it, licking it up with their flames of light, then later shaking gold coins from themselves. By eating the gold coins shaken from the Will o' the Wisps, the Green Snake is able to shine a light from within herself which illuminates her surroundings. It is in the underground Temple of the Kings that we first meet the Old Man with the Lamp. His is a special lamp that can only give light when another light is already present. It is he who first speaks the words, 'The Time has Come!', upon hearing a secret whispered into his ear by the Snake. The tale moves on and we meet the Wife of the Old Man with the Lamp. She leads the story further when she meets a young Prince walking in melancholy mood by the river. He loves the Beautiful Lily, but cannot approach her because, lovely though she is, her touch brings death to all living things, a fate which is deeply distressing to her as well as the Prince. So now we learn the central sorrow and tension of the tale. How will this be overcome?

There are moments at midday, midnight, twilight and dawn when the river can be crossed the other way, back from the sense-perceptible land to the Spirit Land. At midday and midnight the Green Snake transforms her body into a temporary bridge across the river whereas the shadow of a Giant performs the same function at Twilight and Dawn. Through this we are shown that there are two possible ways to cross the river from the Land of the Senses, but only at these special times. The scenes follow one another from midnight to dawn, through midday to twilight and a second midnight, dawn and finally midday when all is resolved. *Seven* stages, that most rhythmical of numbers. By crossing the temporary bridge formed by the Green Snake at midday, the Wife and the young Prince come to the garden of the Beautiful Lily. In this garden, attended by her three handmaidens, we witness the Beautiful Lily sorrowing for her own condition yet bringing joy, wonder and love to all who meet with her. At twilight, when the rich colours of the day gradually die into the night, tragedy befalls the Prince, who, overcome by his desire for the Beautiful Lily, rushes towards her and his life is extinguished by her touch. The Green Snake, who is also present, immediately forms a circle around the Prince, clenching her tail between her teeth. The Old Man with the Lamp reappears as does his Wife and the Will o' the Wisps. Under the guidance of the Man with the Lamp the whole group crosses over the bridge, formed by the Snake at midnight, back into the Land of the Senses. Here remarkable transformations occur. Guided by the Old Man, the Beautiful Lily touches the Snake with her left hand and the Prince with her right, whereby he is brought back to life, but in a dream-like state. The Green Snake changes herself into a pile of precious gems that are then thrown into the river. With the help of the Will o' the Wisps' ability to eat gold, the group re-enters the underground Temple of the Kings. This Temple now magically moves beneath the river, coming up underneath the Ferryman's hut, which falls into the open roof of the Temple and is transformed into a beautiful silver altar inside the Temple. The whole Temple has now arisen from the Earth and stands in the sunlight. The Three Kings of Gold, Silver and Bronze bestow gifts on the Prince that together overcome his dream-like state, restoring his full consciousness and stature. The fourth, 'mixed metal' King has had his gold 'veins' licked away by the Will o' the Wisps and has collapsed. The Prince can now be united in marriage with the Beautiful Lily, for her touch no longer brings death. As King and Queen they look out from the Temple and see that a *permanent* bridge now spans the river across which people are travelling to and fro. This bridge is the result of the sacrifice of the Green Snake, cast as precious stones into the river. Now the two lands are united for all humanity and the final words of the Fairy Tale tell us '…the Bridge, to this day, is swarming with travellers and the Temple is the most frequented in the whole world'.

It is not the purpose of this article to retell the whole story with all its wonderful details, but to look only at a few themes and events that may help to bring alive its relevance for us. Many seemingly small details in this tale hold a world of knowledge and wisdom within them and it is the contemplation of this tale and all it contains which can lead to new and deeper understanding of some of the mysteries of the human soul.

So finally we follow a little more of the destiny of this Fairy Tale, for it brings us to a man who, more than any other, has helped reveal the spiritual wealth contained within it.

In February, 1882, on the occasion of his 28th birthday, Rudolf Steiner (who would later found the spiritual movement of Anthroposophy) received a copy of *The Green Snake and the Beautiful Lily*. It was given to him by Karl Julius Schröer, whom Steiner referred to as his 'teacher and fatherly friend'. Steiner read the tale with interest but could not yet penetrate its deeper meanings, although he returned to it a number of times in the years to come. It lay in Steiner's destiny, after gaining his doctorate at University, to be invited to go to Weimar to edit Goethe's writings on Natural Science. Whilst there, the inner depth of the Fairy Tale began to reveal itself to him. Later, he was to describe how 'it was in the late eighties of the last century that the knot of Goethe's Fairy Tale untied itself for me' and that by understanding how Goethe had arranged the sequence of pictures in the tale, Steiner realized they made possible a transforming power on the soul of the reader. He felt moved to make the profound statement: 'This is the new way to Christ'. A great work of art only reveals itself in its deeper Being to one who is patient, allowing time, not forcing an understanding. This was to be Steiner's experience.

On 27 November, 1891, Steiner spoke about 'The Secret in Goethe's Fairy Tale' at the Goethe Society in Vienna. He later recalled that the Fairy Tale came strongly once more into his inner life in 1896. In the years that followed, according to Steiner's own biography, he went through a tremendous inner struggle with the materialism of the age in which he lived, culminating in him 'standing in the spiritual presence of the Mystery of Golgotha in a most profound and solemn festival of knowledge'. Shortly after this experience, in 1899, Steiner, now 38 years old, wrote an essay to commemorate the 150th anniversary of Goethe's birth, entitled *The Character of Goethe's Spirit as Shown in the Fairy Tale of the Green Snake and the Beautiful Lily* which was published in Berlin in 'The Magazine for literature' during August of that year. A year later, at Michaelmas, 29 September, 1900, Steiner gave a private lecture where he spoke about the Fairy Tale under the title *Goethe's Secret Revelation*

(*Goethe's geheime Offenbarung*). He was later to refer to this as his first anthroposophical lecture. Throughout his life he made mention on many occasions concerning this Fairy Tale. Of course, there were many other influences at work in Steiner's life, but the significance of his relationship to Goethe, his work and particularly the Fairy Tale cannot be overlooked. It is in acknowledging Steiner's insights to this tale that we now return for a look at some of its themes, but perhaps bearing in mind what he said of his own approach to understanding the Fairy Tale, 'I did not write a commentary; I let the living lead me into the living'.

The theme of Goethe's Fairy Tale is the transformation of the soul, which is an alchemical process. The Fairy Tale itself is a piece of alchemy, as Steiner discovered, whereby he was able to state from his own spiritual research that it was a work of art inspired by Rosicrucian wisdom. We may recall that with his illness around the age of 18, Goethe was led into connection with spiritual writings particularly those concerning alchemy. Goethe read, a number of times, a work entitled *The Chymical Wedding of Christian Rosenkreutz: Anno 1459* which was first published in Strasbourg, in 1616. This book contained, in pictorial imaginations, the experience of an initiation in the spiritual worlds. Those serving the Rosicrucian path are concerned with the transformation of substance—both the substance of the human soul and of the earth herself. Matter can be viewed as condensed spirit, darkened light, held fast, 'spell-bound', enchanted into physical form, as it were. When a transforming spiritual impulse can penetrate into matter, the condensed, imprisoned spirit-form can be released anew into pure spirit. The transforming of 'soul substance' is the overcoming of selfish human desires, making the soul a fit vessel for the spirit. Spiritual transformation of substance is the basis of a true alchemy. Goethe's Fairy Tale has an inner architecture that follows alchemical principles. These principles—of separation, purification and re-combining in a new way—can be seen in the tale: the differentiation of the characters and their tasks, the purification through love and sacrifice (which the Green Snake willingly does), then leading to a new community life-condition imbued with spirit. On the way through this process, death occurs, showing the Rosicrucian principle of 'dying in order to become'. This principle Goethe upheld in his own life and creative work. Nature, going through her cycles, readily describes this process with the dying away in autumn and the birth of new life in spring.

Schiller's conceptual thoughts concerning human freedom and the soul forces of the human being became, through Goethe's imaginative creativity, the figures and events in his Fairy Tale. He allowed his imaginative pictures to grow and metamorphose towards the solution to the question: How does the human soul attain to freedom? Steiner maintained that the various figures in the Fairy Tale were supersensibly perceived in Goethe's imagination and therefore are true to themselves—not born from flights of fancy, but coming from the realm of real Imagination, through Goethe, as artistic phantasy. The Beautiful Lily is a picture of the pure spiritual forces, the embodiment of Freedom not accessible to the soul in its normal state, thus the river separating the 'two lands', the one of the spirit where the Beautiful Lily lives and the one of the senses, where the young Prince lives. Unprepared souls die at her touch. This indicates that a soul must be ripe in its powers to be able to *consciously* receive the spirit into it. The Green Snake, who has her home in a cleft in the rocks, is the embodiment of the subterranean forces of the soul. Life on Earth brings experiences to the human soul and the Green Snake is the embodiment of the sum of these experiences which when ripe, when 'The Time has Come', can be sacrificed to form a permanent and fully conscious bridge to the spirit. These two conditions—of Lily and Snake—must be freely united in the soul in order for it to fulfil its true being. (Here we might recall Schiller's threefold picture.) The young Prince is the seeking soul. By the end of the tale, his unity with the Beautiful Lily has come about due to the awakening of previously slumbering soul forces enabling the Prince to unite with Freedom through the sacrifice of his life experience, when the time is ripe, as embodied in the actions of the Green Snake. His earthly life experience has now been transformed, becoming a new inner quality uniting the 'two lands'. This is the new condition of soul that both Schiller and Goethe were striving to experience: the free human personality. This soul transformation, bringing about new human community, is the outcome of the Fairy Tale.

The Old Man with the Lamp has an important role in the whole. He is that soul force which is the guide, knowing when the *time is right* what to do. In the first Temple scene the Gold King asks him about secrets. The Old Man says he knows three. The King then asks which is the most important. The Old Man says he will reveal that when he learns the fourth secret. At that moment the Green Snake approaches and whispers in his ear. Then the Old Man cries out 'The Time has Come!' We do not learn directly in this moment what the Snake has said, but, later in the tale, as she is curled around the dead Prince, she again speaks to the Old Man and tells him that she is willing to sacrifice herself. This she does. Steiner shows that what she whispered to the Old Man in the Temple was her free resolve to sacrifice herself. The Old Man knew that she must make her sacrifice, but he had to wait until she did it of her own free will. Then he could say, 'The Time has Come!'

The Christian path to Love is one of Sacrifice. In the Fairy Tale it is the sacrifice of the loving Green Snake that provides the force to make all things possible. Now we may better understand the title of this Fairy Tale. The Snake and the Lily are the two poles that the striving soul must unite in the right way to gain Freedom for itself. But other forces must also play their part, and we learn that they all receive their transformations at the end of the tale.

Three times in the tale the Old man speaks out 'The Time has Come!' In the Temple, a little while later to his Wife and then again in the Temple with the whole group. Three times the Beautiful Lily hears these words spoken out: by the Wife when she relates events to her, by the Green Snake who also speaks to her and finally in the presence of the Old Man in the final Temple scene. Three is a powerful number; it relates to the Holy Trinity and is always present, in some form, in a true Fairy Tale. Weaving through Goethe's tale, the three cries by the Old Man precipitate action. The three 'hearings' by the Beautiful Lily unite past, present and future into an eternal *now*. Once, twice, thrice! builds a force that must be heard. The Time has Come! This full moment of will for action is the crucible for change. New conditions then appear.

The element of three appears also with the Kings of Gold, Silver and Bronze who bestow gifts on the Prince, bringing him to a full consciousness of his new Kingdom. These three Kings are related to the soul faculties of Thinking, Feeling and Willing, or Doing and their individual gifts strengthen these three, newly separated realms in the Prince. These realms have to become independent in order to work freely with one another within the soul. In the normal human condition they are mixed together, like the fourth King, and bring chaotic conditions into the human soul, making it unfree. This understanding of these three forces working freely in the healthy human soul enabled Steiner, later in his life, to develop a threefold picture of society. He envisaged society as composed of three independent but freely associating realms: the free spiritual-cultural life, the life of equal legal-rights between people, and brotherhood in the economic life. There was a prefiguring of this in the ideals of the French Revolution of Liberty, Equality and Fraternity, but they could not be realized as true social forms because they were viewed from an external perspective and not as qualities coming from the actual soul configuration of the free human personality.

Gold and light also weave together as themes throughout the Fairy Tale. Gold appears both as wisdom, in the Gold King, and money, in the gold coins. It shows two sides of itself in human hands, bringing illumination and wisdom or suffering. When eaten by the Green Snake it causes her to shine light, but when a little dog belonging to the Wife eats some gold coins shaken down by the Will o' the Wisps, it dies. The Old Man's Lamp, when no other light is present, turns stone into gold. It is a wise Light. In the Fairy Tale, light appears in many forms, not least as the waxing and waning of daylight which places events at different times of the day and night. Here we could mention how the temporary bridges of the Green Snake and the Shadow of the Giant relate to the soul's relationship to the spiritual world. These are moments in the Fairy Tale when it is possible to cross over from the Land of the Senses to the Land of the Spirit. In life, art is a bridge to the spirit. In creating art and entering its phantasy, the human being can be free for a moment, in touch with the creative source of things. This is the secret of the Green Snake forming a bridge at midday and midnight, for this enables—just at those moments—a crossing from the Land of the Senses to the Land of the Spirit. The Shadow of the Giant at twilight and dawn is another matter. One can also cross the river by this means, but, as the name 'shadow' implies, it is done not in full consciousness. It happens at twilight or dawn when things are not so definite; it is not clearly day or night as in the midday-midnight moments when the Green Snake makes her temporary bridge. And it is not the Giant who can take people across, only his shadow. There is a dimming of awareness, one which we can understand in our modern times through the experiences people have when access to spiritual experiences is found by the use of drugs, or dubious mediumistic practices and the like. These are not clear paths to the spirit, in conscious knowledge, but access is gained through a 'shadow' of this knowledge.

The reader is invited to approach this Fairy Tale and make his or her own discoveries as well as look further into the wealth of insights that Steiner brought. The tale can be seen as a picture of one human soul. All the figures and events in the tale are the interacting forces within the one, striving, human soul. But within this context the forces have an individual existence, which Goethe's characters give expression to. There are something like 20 characters in this tale. We have looked at some of the elements that exist in it as a means of orientating towards a deeper experience. Ultimately the tale itself should be allowed to reveal its own nature to each reader. Then, perhaps, a living understanding of the tale will also reveal itself, when the time has come!

The Fairy Tale went through its own metamorphosis.

Concerning the question of how the soul can attain freedom and create healthy social forms, Schiller, with his *thinking*, grasped the idea of a way forward. Goethe transformed it through phantasy into the *feeling* life of pictorial imagination. Rudolf Steiner completed this trilogy by transforming the Fairy Tale into a Mystery Drama, performed on the stage; he brought it into the w*ill*. In his autobiography, Steiner said the following: 'The Goethe Fairy Tale images hark back to Imaginations which had often been set forth before the time of Goethe by seekers for the spiritual experience of the soul... not the interpretation, but the stimulus to the experience of the soul was the important result that came to me from my work upon the Fairy Tale. This stimulus later influenced the future life of my soul in the shaping of the mystery dramas I afterwards wrote.'

Originally Steiner had intended to create a dramatic form of Goethe's Fairy Tale, but discovered that it could not happen because 'it was clearly necessary to present these images in a far more concrete manner suited for our time'. And so Steiner metamorphosed the figures of Goethe's Fairy Tale, essentially the different soul forces at work in one human soul, into individual human beings, where one

soul force or another predominates, dealing with life's tensions in
a contemporary setting. This drama he called 'The Portal of Initiation'. It is possible when reading both the Fairy Tale and this Mystery Drama to see which characters belong together. For example,
the Green Snake has become the 'Other Maria' in Steiner's drama, a
self-sacrificing nurse. The Beautiful Lily is 'Maria' who has attained
much in spiritual development and helps a man called Johannes to
also develop further. In him we have Goethe's young Prince. The
Old Man has become Felix Balde, a nature-mystic echoing the qualities of Jacob Boehme (a German mystic of the Middle Ages). And
so on. The characters in this Mystery Drama show the relationship
of karma and destiny in human souls striving to come closer to the
spirit. This Drama was performed in 1910 and Steiner wrote three
more. In the second he drew upon traditions of the Knights Templar.
The third and fourth Steiner claims as purely his own, representing
the workings of anthroposophy. In order to find a permanent home
for the performances of these Dramas a wooden building was created in Dornach, Switzerland. This was burned down in 1923 and a
second building, this time in concrete, grew out of the ashes. They
both bore the name the *Goetheanum* in honour of the man who
had so deeply influenced Steiner's life and had provided the artistic
seed inspiration for his own Mystery Dramas. Steiner was to say that
Goethe's Fairy Tale was the archetypal seed of the anthroposophical movement. Indeed, just as the Green Snake sacrificed herself
to form the bridge, which could permanently unite the 'two lands',
so Steiner gave his life's work to create, through anthroposophy, a
living bridge into the spiritual worlds from our earthly sense-perceptible one. He realized on earth something of the 'Crowning Glory'
of Goethe's Fairy Tale.

In his Mystery Dramas, of which he wrote four, Steiner honoured
the Fairy Tale as a form of artistic expression by having Felix Balde's wife, Felicia (the metamorphosed 'Old Man' and 'Wife' from
Goethe's Fairy Tale) recite Fairy Tales she herself has created. In a
lecture he gave concerning his second Mystery Drama, Steiner had
the following to say: 'In our time there begins that new age in which
it becomes necessary again to find access to higher worlds. For this
a certain transition must be established and it is scarcely possible
to make this transition more simply than by a sensible revival of a

feeling for Fairy Tales. Between that spiritual world to which man can raise himself by clairvoyance and the world of the intellect and the senses, the Fairy Tale is perhaps the truest of all mediums. The very way in which the modest Fairy Tale approaches us, not laying claim in any sense to be an image of external reality but boldly disregarding all outer laws of external realities, makes it possible for the Fairy Tale to prepare the human soul to receive again the higher spiritual world.'

There will always be new things to discover within this tale because any living story, concerned with the verities of human existence, be it called myth, legend or Fairy Tale, has the ability to grow through the ages as a companion to humanity—alive in its own right because they, like us, come out of the spirit's creative source. We may recall that, when Goethe first published the Fairy Tale in the magazine *Die Horen*, it was introduced within a series of stories by the figure of an elderly clergyman who said that he was going to tell a fairy story that would remind them of 'everything and nothing'. And so it is. The Fairy Tale will surely speak to those who are able to hear and say nothing to those who can't.

The last words should now rest with Goethe and his inspired creation, *The Fairy Tale of The Green Snake and the Beautiful Lily.* Early in the Fairy Tale the Gold King asks the Green Snake:

'What is more noble than Gold?'
'Light,' replies the Snake.
'And what is more refreshing than Light?' asks the King.
'Speech,' replies the Snake.

Appendix 2: Mantras of Scene 3 and Scene 7

Scene 3:

The weaving essence of the light streams forth	*Des Lichtes webend Wesen,* es erstrahlet
Through depths of space to fill the world with life;	Durch Raumesweiten Zu fullen die Welt mit Sein;
Love's grace doth warm the centuries of time	Der Liebe Segen, er warmet Die Zietenfolgen
To call forth revelation of all worlds.	Zu Rufen aller Welten Offenbarung.
And spirit-messengers come forth to wed	*Und Geistesboten, sie vermählen*
The weaving essence of creative life	Des Lichtes webend Wesen
With revelations of the souls of men;	Mit Seelenoffenbarung;
And that man, who can wed to both of these	Und wenn vermählen kann mit beiden
His very self, he lives in spirit-heights.	Der Mensch sein eigen Selbst, Ist er in Geisteshöhen lebend.

Prayer

O spirits, who are visible to man,	O Geister, die erschauen kann der Mensch
Quicken with life the soul of this our son.	Belebet unseres Sohnes Seele.

From inmost depths may there stream forth for him	Im Innern lasset ihm erstrahlen,
That which can fill his soul with spirit light.	Was ihm durchleuchten kann Die Seele mit dem Geisteslicht.
From inmost depths may there resound from him	Im Innern lasset ihm ertönen
That which can wholly wake in him his Self	Was ihm erwecken kann
To the creative joy of spirit-life.	Das Selbst zu Geistes Werdelust.

Answer

To founts of worlds primeval	Es steigen seine Gedanken
His surging thoughts do mount	In Urweltgründe
What as shadow he hath thought	Was als Schatten er gedacht
What as fancy he hath lived	Was als Shemen er erlebt,
Soars up beyond the world of form and shape	Entschwebet der Gestaltenwelt,
On whose fullness pondering	Von deren Fülle
Mankind in shadow dreams	Die Menschen denkend In Schatten träumen
O'er whose fullness gazing forth	Von deren Fülle
Mankind in fancy lives	Die Menschen sehend, In Schemen leben.

Scene 7:

The Weaving essence of the light streams forth	Des Lichtes webend Wesen, es erstrahlet
From man to man to fill all worlds with truth.	Von Mensch zu Mensch, Zu füllen alle Welt mit Wahrheit.
The grace of love spreads warmth from soul to soul	Der Liebe Segen, er erwarmet Die Seele an der Seele
To work out bliss eternal for all worlds.	Zu wirken aller Welten Seligkeit.
And spirit-messengers come forth to wed	Und Geistesboten, sie vermählen
Man's works of love and grace to cosmic aims.	Der Menschen Segenswerke Mit Weltenzielen.
And when the man who finds himself in man	Und wenn vermählen kann die beiden
Can wed these twain, there doth stream forth on earth	Der Mensch, der sich im Menschen findet,
True spirit-light from his warm loving soul.	Erstrahlet Geisteslight durch Seelenwäme.

English translations from Harry Collison.

Bibliography

Versions of the Play

Bittleston, Adam: translation of Rudolf Steiner's *The Portal of Initiation*. Rudolf Seiner Publications, New Jersey 1961. Includes Thomas Carlyle's translation of the 'Fairy tale of the Green Snake and the Beautiful Lily'

Collison, Harry: translation of Rudolf Steiner's *Four Mystery Plays,* volumes 1 & 2. Anthroposophical Publishing Co., London 1925

Pusch, Ruth and Hans: translation of *Four Mystery Dramas*. Rudolf Steiner Press, London 1997

Steiner, Rudolf: *Vier Mysteriendramen*. Verlag der Rudolf Steiner-Nachlassverwaltung, Dornach

Other Works

Collison, Harry: *A Commentary on Rudolf Steiner's Plays*, Rudolf Steiner Publishing Co. 1949

Goethe, J.W.: *The Fairy Tale of the Green Snake and the Beautiful Lily*, Garber Communications 1991

Goethe, J.W.: *Italian Journey*, Penguin Classics 1985

Goethe, J.W.: *Wilhelm Meister's Travels; The Recreations of the German Emigrants; The Sorrows of Young Werther; Elective Affinities*, www.forgottenbooks.com

Hutchins, Eileen: *Introduction to the Mystery Plays of Rudolf Steiner*, Rudolf Steiner Press, London 1984

Pusch, Hans: *Working Together on Rudolf Steiner's Mystery Dramas*, Anthroposophic Press, New York 1980

Schiller, Friedrich: *On the Aesthetic Education of Man*, Penguin Classics 2016

By Rudolf Steiner

According to Matthew (Lectures 2, 5, 10 & 12), Anthroposophic Press 2003

Art as Spiritual Activity, Anthroposophic Press 1998

Arts and their Mission, The, Anthroposophic Press 1964

Background to the Gospel of Saint Mark (Lectures 1, 5 & 8), Rudolf Steiner Press 1985

Course of My Life, The, Anthroposophic Press, 1986 (for Felix Koguzki see p. 41)

From Jesus to Christ (Lecture 9), Rudolf Steiner Press 1991

Genesis, Secrets of Creation (Lectures 1, 6 & 11), Rudolf Steiner Press 2002

Goethe's World View, Mercury Press 2004

Influences of Lucifer and Ahriman, The, Anthroposophic Press 1993

Karmic Relationships, Volumes 1-8, Rudolf Steiner Press (for Strader, see Vol. 4, lecture of 18 September 1924)

Knowledge of the Higher Worlds, Rudolf Steiner Press 1969

Outline of Esoteric Science, An, Anthroposophic Press 2002

Reincarnation and Karma, Anthroposophic Press 1992

Rosicrucian Wisdom, Rudolf Steiner Press 2000

Secrets of the Threshold, Rudolf Steiner Press / Anthroposophic Press 1987

Speech and Drama, Anthroposophic Press 2007

Three Lectures on the Mystery Dramas, Anthroposophic Press 1983

Wonders of the World, Ordeals of the Soul, Revelations of the Spirit (Lectures 1, 9 & 10), Rudolf Steiner Press 2020

Notes

Introduction

1. Rudolf Steiner: 'Three Lectures on the Mystery Dramas', p. 38-9.
2. Rudolf Steiner: 'The Arts and their Mission', p. 85, Oslo, in 18 May 1923.

A Portal to a Different Kind of Drama

1. Rudolf Steiner: 'Three Lectures on the Mystery Dramas'. Basel 17 September, 1910, p.1.
2. Rudolf Steiner: 'Three Lectures on the Mystery Dramas'. Berlin 31 October, 1910, p.38.
3. The Prelude, Pusch, p.13.
4. Rudolf Steiner: 'Three Lectures on the Mystery Dramas'. Basel 17 September, 1911, p.25.
5. Scene 7. Pusch, p.108.
6. Ibid, p.111-112.
7. The Interlude. Pusch, p.123.
8. The Prelude. Pusch, p.17.
9. Rudolf Steiner: 'Three Lectures on the Mystery Dramas'. Berlin 31 October, 1910.
10. Scene 3. Pusch, p.68 & p.74.
11. Scene 11. Pusch, p.155.
12. The Prelude. Pusch, p.13.
13. Scene 3. Pusch, p.65.
14. Ibid. p.76.
15. Scene 7. Pusch, p.121.
16. Scene 9. Pusch, p.138.
17. Ibid. Pusch, p. 153.
18. Scene 11. Pusch, p.152.
19. Ibid., p.153.
20. Ibid., p.152.

The Birth of the Portal—A Modern Mystery Drama

1. Harry Collison: *A Commentary on Rudolf Steiner's Four Mystery Plays*, p.13.
2. See my article in *New View*, 2nd Quarter Spring 2016, 'Tragedy'.
3. Clifford Leech, 'Tragedy', Methuen 1969, p.13.
4. Harry Collison: *A Commentary on Rudolf Steiner's Four Mystery Plays*, p.13.
5. Rudolf Steiner: *The Course of My Life*, p.132.
6. Rudolf Steiner: 'Three Lectures on the Mystery Drama', p.37-8.
7. Ibid.
8. Rudolf Steiner: *The Course of My Life*, p.132.
9. Richard Ramsbotham: *New View,* Winter 2020-1, 'The Importance of Freedom and the Future of Culture: Who was the original Johannes Thomasius? Parts 1 & 2.'

The Prelude

1. Hans Pusch: *Working Together on Rudolf Steiner's Mystery Dramas,* pages 2 and 3.
2. The Prelude. Pusch, p.14.
3. The Prelude. Pusch, p.15.
4. The Prelude. Pusch, p.16.
5. The Prelude. Pusch, p.17.
6. Rudolf Steiner: 'Three Lectures on the Mystery Dramas'. p.40-41.

Scene One

1. Scene 1. Pusch, p.26.
2. The Prelude. Pusch, p.18.
3. Scene 1. Pusch, p.26.
4. Scene 1. Pusch, p.52.
5. Scene 1. Pusch, p.25.
6. Scene 1. Pusch, p.27.
7. Scene 1. Collison, p.21.
8. Scene 1. Pusch, p.41.
9. Scene 1. Pusch, p.43.
10. Ibid.
11. Scene 1. Pusch, p.44.
12. Scene 1. Pusch, p.45.

13. Ibid.
14. Scene 1. Pusch, p.46-7.
15. Scene 1. Pusch, p.49-50.
16. See Rudolf Steiner: 'Three Lectures on the Mystery Dramas', p.66, Berlin, 31 October, 1910.
17. Scene 1. Pusch, p.53.
18. Scene 1. Pusch, p.56.

Scene Two
1. Scene 2. Pusch, p.57.
2. Ibid.
3. Scene 2. Pusch, p.58.
4. Ibid.
5. Ibid.
6. Scene 2. Pusch, p.58-9.
7. *A Commentary on Rudolf Steiner's Four Mystery Plays*, p.21.
8. *Four Mystery Plays* Rudolf Steiner, translated by Harry Collison, p.50.
9. Ibid.
10. Ibid, p.51.
11. Ibid.
12. Ibid.
13. Scene 2. Pusch, p.60.
14. Scene 2. Pusch, p.63.
15. Scene 2. Pusch, p.64.

Scene Three
1. Scene 3. Pusch, p.68 & p.73.
2. Eileen Hutchins: *Introduction to the Mystery Plays of Rudolf Steiner*, p.11.
3. Scene 3. Pusch, p.65.
4. The Prelude. Pusch, p.13.
5. Scene 3. Pusch, p.67.
6. Ibid.
7. Scene 3. Pusch, p.68 & p.73.
8. Scene 3. Pusch, p.68-9.
9. Scene 3. Pusch, p.68.
10. Rudolf Steiner: 'According to Matthew', Berne 5.9.1910.

11. Scene 3. Pusch, p.70.
12. Ibid.
13. Harry Collison: *A Commentary on Rudolf Steiner's Four Mystery Plays,* p.24.
14. Scene 3. Pusch, p.73.
15. Ibid.
16. Scene 3. Pusch, p.72.
17. Scene 3. Pusch p.73.
18. Scene 3. Pusch, p.68 & p.73.
19. Scene 3. Pusch, p.74.
20. Scene 3. Pusch, p.75.
21. The English and German versions may be found in Appendix 2.
22. Scene 3. Pusch, p.76.
23. Scene 3. Pusch, p.76-7.
24. Scene 3. Pusch, p.72.

Scene Four

1. Scene 4. Pusch, p.80.
2. Harry Collison: *Four Mystery* Plays, Rudolf Steiner. Volume 1, p.4.
3. For further reading suggestions see Bibliography.
4. Scene 4. Pusch, p.79.
5. Scene 4. Pusch, p.78.
6. Scene 4. Pusch, p.78 & 79.
7. Collison translation (as note 2), p.68.
8. Collison translation (as note 2), p.69.
9. Scene 4. Pusch, p.80.
10. Rudolf Steiner: 'Three Lectures on the Mystery Dramas', p.63. Berlin 31 October, 1910.
11. Ibid.
12. Scene 4. Pusch, p.81.
13. Scene 4. Pusch, p.83-4.
14. Scene 4. Pusch, p.86.
15. Scene 4. Pusch, p.87.
16. Ibid.
17. Scene 4. Pusch, p.88.
18. Scene 4. Pusch, p.89.

19. Scene 4. Pusch, p.87.
20. Scene 4. Pusch. p.88.
21. Ibid.
22. Scene 4. Pusch, p.89.
23. Scene 4. Pusch, p.90.

Scene Five

1. *The Portal of Initiation* by Rudolf Steiner, translated by Adam Bittleston. Scene 5, p.133.
2. Ibid.
3. Bittleston. Scene 5, p.126.
4. 'Three Lectures on the Mystery Dramas', Rudolf Steiner. Berlin, 31 October,1910, p.68.
5. Ibid. p.66-68.
6. Ibid. p.68.
7. Ibid.
8. Bittleston. Scene 5, p.126.
9. Ibid. p.127.
10. Ibid.
11. Ibid.
12. Ibid.
13. Ibid. p.128, also: Harry Collison *A Commentary on Rudolf Steiner's Four Mystery Plays*, the spirits identified on p. 30-1.
14. Bittleston. Scene 5, p.128.
15. Ibid. p. 129.
16. Ibid.
17. Ibid. p.130.
18. Ibid. p.131.
19. Ibid. p.133.
20. Ibid.
21. Ibid.
22. Ibid. p.134.
23. Ibid.
24. Ibid.
25. Ibid.
26. Ibid. p.135.

Scene Six

1.   Scene 6. Pusch, p.103.
2.   Scene 4. Pusch, p.86.
3.   Scene 6. Pusch, p.103.
4.   Ibid.
5.   Ibid.
6.   Scene 6. Pusch, p.102.
7.   Ibid.
8.   Ibid.
9.   Scene 6. Pusch, p.104.
10. Rudolf Steiner: 'Three Lectures on the Mystery Dramas'. Berlin, 31 October, 1910, p.71.
11. Harry Collison: *A Commentary on Rudolf Steiner's Four Mystery Plays*, p.32.
12. Scene 6. Pusch, p.104.
13. Ibid.
14. Rudolf Steiner: 'Harmony of the Creative Word', Dornach, 4 November 1923.
15. Scene 6. Pusch, p.104.
16. Scene 6. Pusch, p.105.
17. Harry Collison: *A Commentary on Rudolf Steiner's Four Mystery Plays*, p.19.
18. Gairman is called 'German' in the German original, and 'Germanus in Collison's translation.
19. Harry Collison: *A Commentary on Rudolf Steiner's Four Mystery Plays*, p.19.
20. Scene 6. Pusch, p.106.
21. Ibid.
22. Scene 6. Pusch, p.107.
23. Ibid.

Scene Seven

1.   Rudolf Steiner: 'Three Lectures on the Mystery Dramas'. Basel, 17 September 1910, p.26.
2.   Ibid. p.26-7.
3.   Scene 7. Pusch, p.109.

4. Rudolf Steiner: 'Three Lectures on the Mystery Dramas'. Basel, 17 September 1910, p.25.

5. Scene 7. Pusch, p.111.

6. Scene 7. Pusch, p.110.

7. Ibid.

8. Scene 7. Pusch, p.109.

9. Rudolf Steiner: 'Harmony of the Creative Word'. Dornach, 2 November 1923, p114.

10. Ibid. p.116.

11. Ibid. p.119.

12. Scene 7. Pusch, p.112-3.

13. Scene 7. Pusch, p.114.

14. Scene 7. Pusch, p.118.

15. Ibid.

16. Scene 7. Pusch, p.120.

17. Rudolf Steiner: 'Three Lectures on the Mystery Dramas'. Basel, 17 September 1910, p.26.

The Interlude

1. *The Interlude*. Pusch, p.125.

2. Ibid, p.124.

3. Ibid.

4. Ibid. p.125.

5. Ibid. p.126.

Scene Eight

1. Scene 8. Pusch, p.133.

2. Scene 3. Pusch, p.68 & p.74.

3. Scene 8. Pusch, p.128.

4. Ibid. p.130.

5. The Interlude. Pusch, p.126.

6. Scene 8. Pusch, p.129.

7. Ibid.

8. Ibid.

9. Ibid.

10. Ibid. p.135.

11. Ibid.
12. Ibid.
13. Ibid. p.131.
14. Ibid.
15. Ibid. p.132.
16. Ibid. p.130.
17. Ibid.
18. Ibid. p.132.
19. Ibid.
20. Ibid. p.134.
21. Ibid. p.133.
22. Ibid.

Scene Nine

1. Scene 9. Pusch, p.139.
2. Scene 9. Pusch, Translator's note, p.136.
3. Steiner refers to Imaginative cognition as being at a lower stage than Intuition and Inspiration.
4. Scene 2. Pusch, p.57.
5. Scene 9. Pusch, p.137.
6. Scene 2. Pusch, p.57.
7. Scene 9. Pusch, p.137.
8. Scene 2. Pusch, p.58.
9. Scene 2. Pusch, p.59.
10. Scene 9. Pusch, p.138.
11. Scene 2. Pusch, p.59.
12. Scene 9. Pusch, p.139.
13. Scene 2. Pusch, p.63.
14. Scene 9. Pusch, p.140-1.
15. Scene 9. Pusch, p.140.
16. Ibid.

Scene Ten

1. Scene 10. Pusch, p. 148.
2. Ibid. p.142.
3. Ibid. p.143.

4. Ibid.

5. Ibid. p.144.

6. Ibid.

7. Ibid. p.145.

8. Ibid.

9. Ibid.

10. Ibid.

11. Ibid. p.146.

12. Ibid.

13. Ibid. p.147.

14. Ibid.

Scene Eleven—The Final Scene

1. Scene 11. Pusch, p.152.

2. Rudolf Steiner: 'Three Lectures on the Mystery Dramas', p.14-15, Basel, 17 September 1910.

3. Eileen Hutchins: *Introduction to the Mystery Plays of Rudolf Steiner*, p.28.

4. Harry Collison: *A Commentary on Rudolf Steiner's Four Mystery Plays*, p.40.

5. Rudolf Steiner: *Four Mystery Plays* translated by Harry Collison, p.4.

6. Scene 11. Pusch, p.150.

7. Scene 1. Pusch, p.30.

8. Scene 11. Pusch, p.151.

9. Ibid.

10. Ibid.

11. Ibid.

12. Ibid.

13. Ibid. p.152.

14. Ibid.

15. Ibid.

16. Ibid.

17. Imaginative cognition is the most basic level. Steiner referred to Imagination, Intuition and Inspiration.

18. Scene 11. Pusch, p. 153.

19. Ibid.

20. Ibid.

21. Ibid.

22. Ibid.

23. Ibid.

24. Ibid. p.154.

25. Ibid.

26. Ibid. p.155.

27. Ibid.

28. Ibid.

The Characters

1.   Scene 1. Pusch, p.26.

Johannes Thomasius

1.   Sc. 1. Pusch, p.52.

2.   Sc. 3. Pusch, p.75.

3.   Sc. 7. Pusch, p.117.

4.   Sc. 7. Pusch, p.117.

5.   Sc. 7. Pusch, p.117.

6.   Sc. 7. Pusch, p.118.

7.   Sc. 8. Pusch, p.135.

8.   See Appendix 2 for the scenes side by side.

9.   Sc. 9. Pusch, p.138.

10. Collison, p.121-125. Bittleston, p.174-179.

11. Sc. 9. Pusch, p.141.

12. Sc. 11. Pusch, p.152.

13. Sc. 11. Pusch, p.154.

Maria

1.   Harry Collison: *A Commentary on Rudolf Steiner's Four Mystery Plays*, p.23.

2.   Scene 3. Pusch, p.73.

3.   *Working Together on Rudolf Steiner's Mystery Dramas*, by Hans Pusch. See p. 34 &36.

4.   Scene 3. Pusch, p.69.

5.   Scene 3. Pusch, p.70.

6.   Ibid.

7.   Harry Collison: *A Commentary on Rudolf Steiner's Four Mystery Plays*, p.24.

8. Scene 3. Pusch, p.67.
9. Scene 3. Pusch, p.68.
10. Harry Collison: *A Commentary on Rudolf Steiner's Four Mystery Plays*, p.23.
11. Rudolf Steiner: *According to Matthew*, p.83, Lecture 5. Basel 5 September 1910.
12. Ibid.
13. Scene 3. Pusch, p.71. Scene 7. Pusch, p.119.
14. Scene 8. Pusch, p.130.
15. Scene 8. Pusch, p.133.
16. Scene 8. Pusch, p.134.
17. Scene 8. Pusch, p.135.
18. Scene 8. Pusch, p.133.
19. Scene 9. Pusch, p.140.

Philia, Astrid and Luna

1. Rudolf Steiner: 'Three Lectures on the Mystery Dramas', p.26. Basel, 17 September 1910.
2. Ibid. p.75. Berlin, 31 October 1910.
3. For information on the nature spirits see, 'Harmony of the Creative Word', Lectures 7, 8 and 9.
4. Scene 1. Pusch, p.26.
5. Scene 1. Pusch, p.31.
6. Scene 1. Pusch, p.33.
7. Ibid.
8. Scene 1. Pusch, p.39.
9. 'The Green Snake and the Beautiful Lily'. See *The Portal of Initiation*, translated by Adam Bittleston, p.220.
10. Rudolf Steiner: 'Three Lectures on the Mystery Dramas', p.25. Basel 17 September 1910.
11. Scene 1. Pusch, p.25.
12. Scene 11. Pusch, p. 152-3.

The Other Maria

1. Scene 4. Pusch, p.88.
2. Scene 1. Pusch, p.47-8.
3. Scene 1. Pusch, p.46-7.

4. Scene 11. Pusch, p.152.
5. Rudolf Steiner, 'Three Lectures on the Mystery Dramas', p.64. Berlin 31 October 1910.
6. Scene 4. Pusch, p.87.
7. Scene 4. Pusch, p.88.
8. See note 5.
9. Rudolf Steiner, 'Three Lectures on the Mystery Dramas', p.64. Berlin 31 October 1910.
10. Ibid.
11. Scene 5. Pusch, p.94-5.
12. Scene 5. Pusch, p.98.
13. Scene 11. Pusch, p.152.
14. Scene 11. Pusch, p.151.

Capesius and Strader

1. Scene 4. Pusch, p.83.
2. See 'The Karma of Anthroposophy', especially Lecture 3, Arnheim 18.9.1924.
3. Scene 4. Pusch, p.86.
4. Ibid.
5. Scene 1. Pusch, p.41.
6. Scene 4. Pusch, p.85.
7. Scene 4. Pusch, p.82.
8. Scene 4. Pusch, p.83.
9. Scene 4. Pusch, p.87.
10. Scene 4. Pusch, p.83.
11. Scene 4. Pusch, p.89.
12. Ibid.
13. Ibid.
14. Scene 4. Pusch, p.90.
15. Scene 8. Pusch, p.132.
16. Scene 8. Pusch, p.134.
17. Scene 11. Pusch, p.149.
18. Scene 11. Pusch, p.150.
19. Scene 11. Pusch, p.155.
20. Ibid.

Felix Balde

1. Scene 5. Pusch, p.97.
2. Scene 1. Pusch, p.40.
3. Scene 1. Pusch, p.40.
4. Scene 1. Pusch, p.42.
5. Ibid.
6. Rudolf Steiner: *The Course of My Life*, p.42.
7. Ibid.
8. Ibid.
9. Scene 1. Pusch, p.43.
10. Harry Collison: *A Commentary on Rudolf Steiner's Four Mystery Plays*, p.18.
11. Scene 5. Pusch, p.95.
12. Scene 5. Pusch, p.93-4.
13. Scene 5. Pusch, p.96.
14. Ibid.
15. Scene 5. Pusch, p.97.
16. Scene 11. Pusch, p.153.
17. Ibid.
18. Scene 11. Pusch, p.154.

Felicia Balde

1. Scene 5. Pusch, p. 103.
2. This is shown in *The Soul's Probation*, in which she is the foster mother of his daughter in the incarnation of the Middle Ages.
3. See W.B. Yeats, *The Celtic Twilight*.
4. Scene 11. Pusch, p.154.
5. Scene 5. Pusch, p.103.
6. Harry Collison, *A Commentary on Rudolf Steiner's Four Mystery Plays*, p. 28-9.
7. Scene 5. Pusch, p.104.
8. Harry Collison, *A Commentary on Rudolf Steiner's Four Mystery Plays*, p.32.
9. Scene 5. Pusch, p.104.
10. Ibid.
11. Ibid.
12. Scene 5. Pusch, p.106.

Theodora
1. Scene 1. Pusch, p.37.
2. Scene 1. Pusch, p.33.
3. *Introduction to the Mystery Plays of Rudolf Steiner*, Eileen Hutchins, p.6.
4. Scene 1. Pusch, p.34.
5. Scene 3. Pusch, p.67.
6. Scene 11. Pusch, p.155.
7. Wood quotes: GA52 p.294, GA 54 p.387 and GA 33 p.305.

Benedictus
1. Scene 3. Pusch, p.85 and p.74.
2. Scene 1. Pusch, p.42.
3. Scene 3. Pusch, p.73.
4. Scene 3. Pusch, p.75.
5. Harry Collinson. *A Commentary on Rudolf Steiner's Four Mystery Plays*, p.24.
6. Scene 5. Pusch, p.92.
7. Scene 5. Pusch, p.99.
8. Ibid.
9. Ibid.

Theodosius, Romanus and Retardus
1. Scene 5. Pusch, p.92.
2. Ibid.
3. Scene 5. Pusch, p.93.
4. Scene 5. Pusch, p.99.
5. Scene 1. Pusch, p.45.
6. Rudolf Steiner: 'Three Lectures on the Mystery Dramas', p.66-8.
7. Scene 1. Pusch, p.50.
8. Ibid.
9. Ibid.
10. Rudolf Steiner: 'Three Lectures on the Mystery Dramas', p.68.
11. Scene 11. Pusch, p.150.
12. Scene 11. Pusch, p.149.
13. Scene 11. Pusch, p.155.
14. Scene 11. Pusch, p.152.
15. Ibid.

16. Ibid.

17. Scene 11. Pusch, p.153.

Lucifer and Ahriman

1. Scene 4. Pusch, p.78.

2. Scene 4. Pusch, p.79.

3. Harry Collison: *Four Mystery Plays,* Vol. 1, p.4.

4. Ibid.

5. Estella's accusation in 'The Prologue'. Pusch, p.17.

6. Scene 4. Pusch, p.79.

7. Ibid.

8. Scene 10. Pusch, p.146.

9. Comparison of the two speeches of Lucifer and Ahriman in scenes four and ten is afforded in Appendix 2.

10. Scene 4. Pusch, p.79.

11. Scene 10. Pusch, p.147.

12. Ibid.

13. Harry Collison: *A Commentary on Rudolf Steiner's Four Mystery Plays*, p.39.

14. Scene 11. Pusch, p.151.

Gairman (or Germanus)

1. Scene 6. Pusch, p.106.

2. Harry Collison: *A Commentary on Rudolf Steiner's Four Mystery Plays* p.19.

3. Scene 1. Pusch, p.50.

4. Scene 1. Pusch, p.51.

5. 'Three Lectures on the Mystery Dramas', Rudolf Steiner, p.71.

6. Ibid.

7. Adam Bittleston: The *Portal of Initiation*, p.237 (Thomas Carlyle's translation of 'The Green Snake and the Beautiful Lily').

8. Ibid.

The Spirit of the Elements

1. Scene 4. Pusch, p.82.

2. Eileen Hutchins: *Introduction to the Mystery Plays of Rudolf Steiner*, p.14.

3. Scene 4. Pusch, p.81.
4. Harry Collison, *Four Mystery Plays*, Rudolf Steiner, Volume 1, p.69.
5. Harry Collison, *Four Mystery Plays*, Rudolf Steiner, Volume 1, p.5.
6. Scene 4. Pusch, p.80.
7. Scene 4. Pusch, p.83 and Scene 1. Pusch, p.44-5.
8. Scene 4. Pusch, p.83.
9. Scene 6. Pusch, p.102.

Appendix 1

1. I make no claims to originality, but record a debt of gratitude to those who have devoted study, research and no little insight into Goethe's life and his creative work of the Fairy Tail. In particular, Paul Marshall Allen and Joan deRis Allen (see *The Time is at Hand!*, Anthroposophic Press 1995).